CW01197777

ClearRevise®

AQA GCSE
Design and Technology 8552

Exam tutor and practice

Published by
PG Online Limited
The Old Coach House
35 Main Road
Tolpuddle
Dorset
DT2 7EW
United Kingdom

sales@pgonline.co.uk
www.clearrevise.com
www.pgonline.co.uk
2023

PG ONLINE

ACKNOWLEDGMENTS

The questions in this textbook are the sole responsibility of the authors and have neither been provided nor approved by the examination board.

Every effort has been made to trace and acknowledge ownership of copyright. The publishers will be happy to make any future amendments with copyright owners that it has not been possible to contact. The publisher would like to thank the following companies and individuals who granted permission for the use of their images or content in this textbook.

Images: © Shutterstock

Design and artwork: Jessica Webb / PG Online Ltd
First edition 2023. 10 9 8 7 6 5 4 3 2 1
A catalogue entry for this book is available from the British Library
ISBN: 9781910523902

Printed on FSC® certified paper by Bell and Bain Ltd, Glasgow, UK.

CONTENTS AND CHECKLIST

3.1: Section A

3.2: Section B

3.3: Section C

COMMAND WORDS

Command words are the words and phrases used in exams and other assessment tasks that indicate how you should answer the question.

Analyse	Separate information into components to identify their characteristics
Apply	Put into effect in a recognised way
Argue	Present a reasoned case
Calculate	Work out the value of something
Compare	Identify similarities and differences
Complete	Finish a task by adding to given information
Consider	Review and respond to given information
Contrast	Identify differences
Define	Specify meaning
Describe	Set out characteristics
Discuss	Present key points about different ideas, or strengths and weaknesses of an idea
Evaluate	Judge from available evidence
Examine	Investigate closely
Explain	Set out purpose or reasons
Give	Produce an answer from recall
How (far)	Work out the correct answer
Identify	Name or otherwise characterise
Justify	Support a case with evidence
Name	Give the correct title or term
Outline	Set out the main characteristics
Repeat (the pattern)	Maths specific; repeat a given pattern
State	Express clearly and briefly
What (is)	Give the correct information
Which	Select or give the correct information

WHAT MAKES THIS GUIDE SPECIAL?

This guide is your personal exam tutor. It offers you a complete walk-through of the specification and related questions in a convenient format.

The best way to ace an exam is to practise... but that doesn't mean just endlessly doing past exam papers.

Imagine you were going to run a 100-metre race. If you really wanted to win it, you'd need a coach. They would analyse how you run and give you advice and lots of little improvements that you could make to win. Of course, you'd do some practice runs, but without coaching, you would have little idea how to improve.

Section 1

1

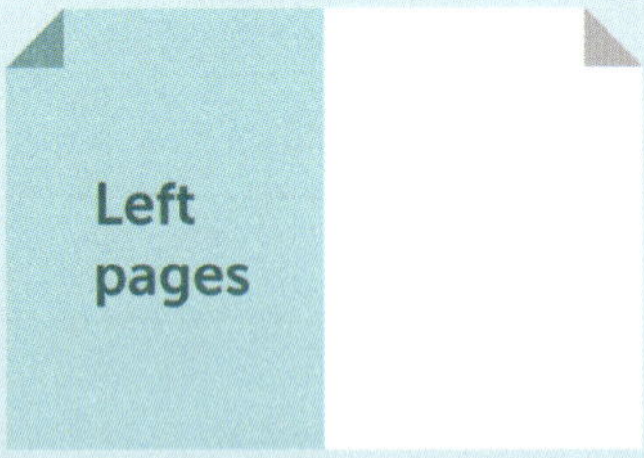

Study questions with model answers

Start on the **left-hand pages**. Left-hand pages coach you through each topic area on the specification. We show you some questions and model answers that would get full marks. We also give you exam tips on exactly what the examiner is looking for from the question or question type.

2

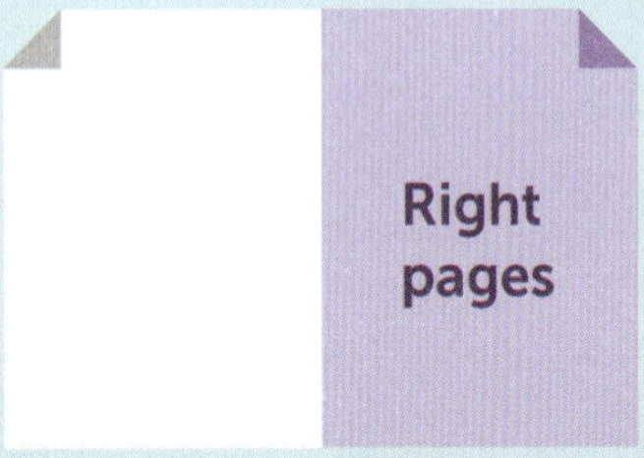

Apply your understanding to related topics

Now it is your turn! Once you have finished looking at the model answers on the left, **right-hand pages** provide you with a set of similar exam questions on the same topic. You should do really well in these as you've just seen model responses and tips on related questions.

3

[1]

✓

Learn from the mark schemes

Mark your work using the mark scheme provided at the bottom of each page.

By the end of Section 1, you will have gone through lots of model answers and had a go at questions on every topic in the entire specification.

If you still feel that a topic needs more work, just use the smile icons ☺ or make a note on the page so that you can look up the topic later or ask your teacher for help.

Section 2

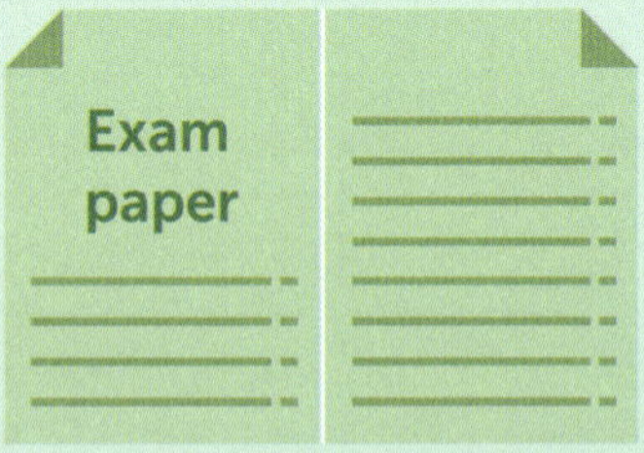

Complete a full practice exam paper

Now is your chance to have a go at a real exam paper. You need to attempt 100 marks in 120 minutes, so allow yourself around 1 mark per minute, plus 20 minutes at the end for improving any sketches, adding annotation to diagrams and correcting those silly mistakes we all tend to make.

When you take the paper, make sure you have a clear desk, turn off your phone and find somewhere quiet. Give yourself the same amount of time as a real exam.

Once you've completed the paper, the answers are in the back of the book for you to mark yourself. Good luck!

THE SCIENCE OF REVISION

'Low stakes' examination practice

Practising past examination questions is a powerful way to revise and improve your understanding of the subject. Mark schemes and professional guidance provide valuable information too. Without the added pressure of the big day and the stressful atmosphere that an exam hall may create, studying all of this in a calm atmosphere where the results don't matter to anyone but yourself, creates the most effective environment for the retrieval of information.

Retrieval of information

Retrieval practice encourages students to come up with answers to questions.[1] The closer the question is to one you might see in a real examination, the better. Also, the closer the environment in which a student revises is to the 'examination environment', the better. Research shows that students who had a test 2–7 days away did 30% better using retrieval practice than students who simply read, or repeatedly reread material. Students who were expected to teach the content to someone else after their revision period did better still.[2] What was found to be most interesting in other studies is that students using retrieval methods and testing for revision were also more resilient to the introduction of stress.[3]

Feedback and note-taking

The tips and advice included with each model answer constructively focus purely on how to get more out of each question or type of question. Every topic shows model questions and answers, along with advice from experienced teachers and opportunities for students to try further similar questions. Answers and tips are displayed on the same page allowing for immediate feedback.[4] There is space for notes – use this if you need to. Making summarised points at the end of a revision session is the most effective way to use notes.[4]

Ebbinghaus' forgetting curve and spaced learning

Ebbinghaus' 140-year-old study examined the rate in which we forget things over time. The findings still hold true. However, the act of forgetting facts and techniques and relearning them is what cements things into the brain.[5] Spacing out revision is more effective than cramming – we know that, but students should also know that the space between revisiting material should vary depending on how far away the examination is. A cyclical approach is required. An examination 12 months away necessitates revisiting covered material about once a month. A test in 30 days should have topics revisited every 3 days – intervals of roughly a tenth of the time available.[6]

Summary

Students: the more tests and past questions you do, in an environment as close to examination conditions as possible, the better you are likely to perform on the day. If you prefer to listen to music while you revise, tunes without lyrics will be far less detrimental to your memory and retention. Silence is most effective.[5] If you choose to study with friends, choose carefully – effort is contagious.[7]

1. Roediger III, H. L., & Karpicke, J.D. (2006). Test-enhanced learning: Taking memory tests improves long-term retention. *Psychological Science*, 17(3), 249–255.
2. Nestojko, J., Bui, D., Kornell, N. & Bjork, E. (2014). Expecting to teach enhances learning and organisation of knowledge in free recall of text passages. *Memory and Cognition*, 42(7), 1038–1048.
3. Smith, A. M., Floerke, V. A., & Thomas, A. K. (2016) Retrieval practice protects memory against acute stress. *Science*, 354(6315), 1046–1048.
4. Kluger, A & DeNisi, A. (1996). The effects of feedback interventions on performance. Psychological bulletin, 119(2), 254–284.
5. Perham, N., & Currie, H. (2014). Does listening to preferred music improve comprehension performance? *Applied Cognitive Psychology*, 28(2), 279–284.
6. Cepeda, N. J., Vul, E., Rohrer, D., Wixted, J. T. & Pashler, H. (2008). Spacing effects in learning a temporal ridgeline of optimal retention. *Psychological Science*, 19(11), 1095–1102.
7. Busch, B. & Watson, E. (2019), *The Science of Learning*, 1st ed. Routledge.

HOW TO FIX MISTAKES IN YOUR EXAM

We all make mistakes, and the chances are that you'll make one or two in the exam.

If you realise that you've made a mistake in an answer, it's no problem.

Cross the answer out so that it is obvious that it's a mistake.

Example 1 – Put a line through the incorrect answer:

1.1 Name **one** smart material [1]

~~Carbon fibre~~ *Shape memory alloy (Nitinol)*

Example 2 – Put a line through each incorrect word.

1.2 Explain how a cam and a follower work in a mechanism.
Name **one** specific cam in your answer. [3]

A cam is a component that rotates about an axis. They are different shapes e.g., ~~pointy cam~~ pear shaped cam. As the cam rotates, the edge of the cam ~~rotates~~ lifts the follower up and down.

Example 3 – Put a cross through a section of writing.

1.3 Explain the term 'anthropometrics'. [2]

~~*Anthropometrics is about the human body and our different organs. It is where we consider how different organs function in the body.*~~

Anthropometrics is about the measurement of the human body and sizes of limbs like your hands (how wide they are) or legs (how long they are). Anthropometrics is not about the internal workings of the body. That is biology.

But DON'T scrub out answers:

What is meant by product analysis? Give an example. [2]

[redacted]

Exam tip

If you cross out an answer but don't write anything else, the examiner is allowed to mark it. But they can't mark it if they can't read it because you scrubbed it out.

SECTION A

3.1 CORE TECHNICAL PRINCIPLES

Information about the paper

Written exam: 2 hours

50% of the qualification

100 marks in total. There are 20 for Section A, 30 for Section B and 50 for Section C.

At least 15% of the exam will assess maths and at least 10% will assess science. All questions are mandatory.

All dimensions are in millimetres.

!

You **will** need:
A black pen (and some spares)

You may also use:
An HB pencil, ruler and other normal writing and drawing instruments
A calculator
A protractor

3.1.1

NEW AND EMERGING TECHNOLOGIES

INDUSTRY AND ENTERPRISE

(1) Start on the left hand page.

(2) Left pages contain example questions with model answers. The answers will get full marks.

01 Which **one** of the following statements best describes fair trade?

A A business owned and managed by its workers ○

B A large number of people who raise money for a project ○

C An organisation that helps workers have decent work and pay conditions ●

D The use of digital and social media in advertising ○

[1]

Exam tip

Aim to eliminate three of the answers to help confirm your choice. For example, answer **D** is the definition of virtual marketing.

Exam tip

The first 10 questions on the exam paper will be MCQs (Multiple Choice Questions).

For each question, completely fill in the circle alongside the appropriate answer.

If you want to change your answer you must cross out your original answer as shown.

If you wish to return to an answer previously crossed out, ring the answer you now wish to select as shown.

02 Define what is meant by the term 'automation'.

Automation allows for repetitive tasks to be carried out by machines rather than by humans.

[1]

Exam tip

Define based questions require you to specify the meaning of a key word.

Do you remember?

Enterprise means to identify business opportunities and make them commercially successful. Manufacturing businesses may use specific tools and equipment to produce their goods and arrange their production line and buildings to optimise efficiency.

Do you remember?

A cooperative is a company that is owned and managed by those that work there.

Crowdfunding may be used to raise money from the public for a new project.

(3) Do you remember boxes may also contain other points on the specification which you need to revise before attempting the questions on the right.

Write your mark here

4 Look at the right-hand page and have a go at some exam style questions on the same topic. The questions below are worth three marks, so you should be able to finish them in three minutes.

03 Which **one** of the following statements is an advantage of using robots?

- **A** Can work in dangerous or harmful environments ☐
- **B** Cannot handle unexpected situations ☐
- **C** Expensive to set up ☐
- **D** Requires a specialist workforce to operate and maintain ☐

[1]

04 A co-operative is:

- **A** A joint venture between two enterprises ☐
- **B** A trade union ☐
- **C** An enterprise owned and run by its workforce ☐
- **D** An enterprise where everyone is paid the same wage ☐

[1]

05 Define the term 'crowd funding'.

....

....

[1]

5 Cover the answers with a sheet of paper so that you're not tempted to cheat!

6 Mark yourself
Once you've finished the questions, mark them using the answers at the bottom of the page.

7 Are you confident? Fill in one of the faces to show whether you feel you did well in the topic or if it needs more revision.

Total

/ 3

☹ 😐 ☺

Answers

03 A. Can work in dangerous or harmful environments.[1]

04 C. An enterprise owned and run by its workforce.[1]

05 Crowd funding involves many small investors putting in capital to fund a new project or business venture.[1]

3.1.1

NEW AND EMERGING TECHNOLOGIES
SUSTAINABILITY AND PEOPLE

01 A finite resource is: **[1]**

A A renewable resource ☐

B A resource that can be replenished ☐

C A resource that grows naturally ☐

D A resource that will eventually run out ☒

Do you remember?

Non-finite resources are in abundant supply and unlikely to run out. These include solar power, wind, wave and tidal energy, timbers and cotton.

02 Define the term 'market pull'. **[1]**

Market pull is when products are designed in response to a market force or consumer need.

Exam tip

Define questions ask you to give a specific meaning.

03 Explain **one** technological change that has made it easier for people to work from home. **[2]**

People now find it easier to work from home as electronic communication platforms using video-conferencing allow people to be connected without meeting face to face. People can now fit their daily lives around social challenges like childcare as they do not have to travel to a permanent place of work.

Exam tip

Explain questions require you to set out a purpose or give reasons for something. Here you should provide one factor for change and then give a reason for why it has caused a change for the second mark to be awarded.

Use any blank space to make notes.

04 Define the term 'technology push'.

....

....

[1]

05 Waste disposal sites collect and sort materials for recycling.

Explain **one** reason why materials are recycled.

....

....

....

....

[2]

06 Explain **one** reason why increased automation in manufacturing has led to a reduction in manufacturing jobs.

....

....

....

....

[2]

Total

/ 5

Answers

04 Technological discoveries are used to drive the development of a product.[1]

05 Finite resources are running out.[1] */ Recycling saves resources which may no longer be available for use in newer products.*[1] *Reduces energy or pollution associated with extraction and processing of raw materials.*[1]

06 Increased technology has led to the use of robots[1] *and automation which replace some workers*[1] *to make goods and products more rapidly and consistently.*[1]

3.1.1

NEW AND EMERGING TECHNOLOGIES

CULTURE AND SOCIETY

01 Define what is meant by the term 'culture'.

Culture is defined as a mixture of fashions, trends, faiths, beliefs, customs and behaviours amongst a group of people.

[1]

02 Explain **one** reason why it is important for designers to ensure new products are inclusive.

Designers should consider all potential users regardless of age, gender or ability to ensure the product is accessible for use by as wide a market as possible, to increase potential sales.

[2]

Exam tip

Remember that there are two parts to **explain** questions. There should be an initial point along with a reason or linked point for justification.

You will find the following connectives will help when answering explain questions:

- ... because ...
- ... as ...
- ... so that ...
- ... which means ...
- ... therefore ...

03 Describe how prosthetic limbs can improve the quality of life for disabled people.

Prosthetic limbs can help people with disabilities with their mobility e.g. walking unaided and in competitive sports e.g., running and competitive events like the Invictus Games and Paralympics.

[2]

Do you remember?

When we talk about society, we consider how designs impact and can improve life for:

- elderly people
- disabled people
- children
- different religious groups.

04 **Figure 1** shows a child's wooden toy based on the Christian story of Noah's Ark.

Figure 1

Explain **one** reason why the child's wooden toy may not sell well in some countries.

....

....

....

[2]

05 Fashion in design means:

A A trend or the way a product looks or is used ⬭

B A unique experience of a person ⬭

C The belief of a person ⬭

D The custom of a person ⬭

[1]

06 Explain how different features on a telephone could be adapted to be more inclusive of older people.

....

....

....

[2]

Total

/ 5

☹ 😐 ☺

Answers

04 A toy based on a story from Christianity may not sell well in countries where other religions are followed[1] as people may not want to promote stories from other faiths and beliefs to their children.[1]

05 A. A trend or the way a product looks or is used.[1]

06 A telephone with larger buttons and large numbers[1] makes them easier to touch[1] and see[1] by an older person with sight issues. A brighter screen with a clear resolution would help too.[1] Gaps between each button will stop fingers with limited movement from hitting the wrong button.[1] Flashing light on ringing for the deaf.[1] Louder ring tone / speaker for the deaf.[1] Hearing loop technology for use with hearing aids.[1]

3.1.1

NEW AND EMERGING TECHNOLOGIES

ENVIRONMENT, PRODUCTION TECHNIQUES AND SYSTEMS

01 Give **two** ways in which manufacturers can reduce their carbon footprint during the manufacture of products.

1. *Use renewable energy.*

2. *Use more recycled materials.*

[2]

Exam tip

Give questions are testing basic knowledge recall. Therefore, they only require a few words or a simple sentence per mark.

02 Define the term 'continuous improvement'.

Continuous improvement is a process where the manufacturer of a product will regularly make small improvements or refinements to make it the best it can be.

[1]

03 Explain **one** benefit of applying the principles of lean manufacturing in industry.

Lean manufacturing focuses on reducing waste and improving efficiency, which results in cost savings and a reduction in the use of materials and resources.

[2]

Do you remember?

Continuous improvement and lean manufacturing are both examples of increasing efficiency in the workplace to reduce costs and save time.

Automation can also improve efficient working as robots can work at a constant rate without human errors, the need for salaries or rest breaks.

Do you remember?

- **CAD** stands for Computer-Aided Design which means designing products using a computer.
- **CAM** stands for Computer-Aided Manufacture and includes computer guided cutting and printing tools.
- **FMS** stands for Flexible Manufacturing Systems. FMS systems are used for short production runs where machinery needs to be adapted to accommodate different product specifications for each run.
- **JIT** stands for Just-in-Time. Stock is ordered and delivered to a manufacturer as it is needed to increase efficiency. Delays in delivery can halt manufacture and costs may be higher as the business is not ordering in bulk quantities.

04 Give **one** way in which burning fossil fuels contributes to global warming.

....

....

[1]

05 Define the term 'Flexible manufacturing system'.

....

....

[1]

06 Give **two** advantages of Just in Time manufacturing.

....

....

....

[2]

07 Explain how the continuous improvement of mobile phone technology may lead to increased pollution.

....

....

....

[2]

Total

/ 6

☹ 😐 ☺

Answers

04 Burning fossil fuels releases CO_2 and other pollutants that are causing global warming.[1]

05 FMS is a method of production that can be easily adapted to change the quantity or type of product/s being manufactured.[1]

06 Products are made to order, saving storage space.[1] Stock doesn't become old or out of date.[1] More factory space can be utilised for other activities.[1] Materials and components are ordered as needed, keeping cash flow in control.[1]

07 Adding features to phones increases power consumption, requiring bigger or better batteries[1] e.g. lithium batteries.[1] Mining the resources used in battery technology damages the environment / pollutes the atmosphere[1] during refinement and processing.[1]

3.1.1

NEW AND EMERGING TECHNOLOGIES

HOW THE CRITICAL EVALUATION OF NEW AND EMERGING TECHNOLOGIES INFORMS DESIGN DECISIONS

01 Explain **one** way in which 'design for maintenance' allows for the life of a product to be extended.

Parts that get worn out or break can be replaced which means the life of the product can be extended rather than being disposed of.

[2]

02 Some manufacturers use planned obsolescence in their product designs.
State what is meant by 'planned obsolescence'.

Planned obsolescence is an approach taken by companies to ensure that a version of a product will become out of date or worn out after a predetermined length of time.

[1]

Exam tip

State type questions simply require you to express your answer clearly and briefly.

Do you remember?

Many manufacturers now make products so that they can be disassembled at the end of their useful working life.

This, and 'take back' schemes are considered a more ethical approach than planned obsolescence.

Do you remember?

The WEEE regulations require UK businesses to:

- Minimise waste from their electrical equipment and promote reuse.
- Ensure waste products are recycled correctly and meet the materials' recovery targets.
- Design products by reducing material use.

01 Some high street electronics retailers offer a 'take back' service whereby they will take back products they sold from customers who no longer require the product or if it is broken.
Explain **one** advantage for the environment of high street shops offering 'take back' schemes.

Stores that take back products prevent old or unwanted electronics from being sent to landfill, in line with WEEE regulations. This means that the product can be broken down into separate material groups and recycled, or the product can be repaired, giving it a new lease of life with another owner.

[2]

04 Explain **one** reason why manufacturers use planned obsolescence in their products.

....

....

[2]

05 Give **two** benefits for the environment of consumers being able to maintain and repair products at home.

1. ....

....

2. ....

....

[2]

06 Explain **one** reason why manufacturers should have to produce goods that can be easily disassembled at the end of their useful working life.

....

....

....

[2]

Figure 1

07 Figure 1 shows a symbol.
State what the symbol means.

....

[1]

Total

/ 7

Answers

04 Consumers will have to buy an upgrade or replacement[1] therefore the company will continue to make a profit.[1]

05 Products do not end up in landfill[1] / there will be less demand for new resources to be extracted, conserving those we have[1] / less waste needing to be incinerated resulting in less pollution.[1]

06 Products should be able to be separated into their different material groups so they can be recycled / reused[1] meaning less waste is sent to landfill.[1]

07 It is the WEEE regulations symbol meaning products with this symbol cannot go in a household waste bin.[1]

3.1.2 ENERGY GENERATION AND STORAGE

01 State **one** type of fossil fuel.

Oil.

[1]

Exam tip

- This question only asks for one type of fossil fuel so you should only give one type as the answer.
- There are, however, three possible correct answers to this question including gas and coal.

02 Fossil fuels are a cost effective and reliable source of energy.
Explain **one** disadvantage of using fossil fuels to generate energy.

They are finite resources which means they will eventually run out.

[2]

03 Explain how nuclear power is generated.

The nuclear material is split in a reactor which in turn produces a great deal of heat. This heats water that turns into steam which drives a generator to produce electricity.

[2]

Do you remember?

Fossil fuels are finite resources, meaning they will eventually run out. Energy is generated from **fossil fuels** and **biomass** in much the same way as it is from nuclear materials except that the raw materials are burned to generate heat to drive a steam turbine.

Renewable energy commonly relies on natural forces or movement to turn a turbine attached to a generator.

Do you remember?

Energy cannot be destroyed but it can be stored in several ways. These include batteries and kinetic pumped storage systems which pump and hold water in a dam that can be released to generate immediate power as it falls. This is how hydroelectric power (HEP) is produced.

Do you remember?

Other disadvantages of using fossil fuels to generate energy include:

- They contain high amounts of carbon which contributes to global warming when being burned.
- They are not sustainable.
- They come with significant associated risks such as potential explosions, spills and environmental contamination.

04 Energy can be stored using kinetic pumped storage systems.
Give **one** other method of storing energy.

....

[1]

05 Explain **one** disadvantage of using wind power to generate energy.

....

....

....

[2]

06 Explain how energy is generated from tidal power.

....

....

....

[2]

07 Give **one** advantage and **one** disadvantage of the use of nuclear power.

Advantage: ....

....

Disadvantage: ....

....

[2]

Total /7

Answers

04 *Alkaline batteries,[1] re-chargeable batteries,[1] flywheel storage.[1]*

05 *The wind does not always blow[1] which means that there is no constant / guaranteed supply of power.[1]*
The turbines might be a long way from the national grid[1] which means there will be high additional costs involved to connect to them.[1]
Wind turbines are huge[1] which some people consider to be unsightly and spoil the landscape.[1]

06 *As the tide comes in and out, water passes through a series of turbines[1] which in turn drive dynamos or generators to produce electricity.[1]*

07 *Award one mark for each. Max one advantage and one disadvantage.[1]*

Advantages	Disadvantages
Does not contribute to global warming / clean energy	Hazardous waste to dispose of / not safe for 1000s of years
Limitless source of power	Very expensive to build a nuclear power plant in terms of time, money and energy
A way of slowing climate change	Very dangerous if an accident happens involving radioactive material

3.1.3 DEVELOPMENTS IN MODERN AND SMART MATERIALS

01 **Figure 1** shows a table containing a list of new materials.

Tick (✓) **one** box in each row to show which group each of the materials belongs to.

Material	Modern material	Smart material
Liquid crystal displays (LCDs)	✓	
Photochromic materials		✓
Graphene	✓	

Figure 1

[3]

Exam tip

In **tick** questions, carefully check the number of boxes that must be ticked in each row.

- For this question, if you tick more than one box in a row you will not get a mark for the row.

02 Give **two** applications for shape memory alloys (SMAs).

SMAs have been used in dental applications to straighten teeth.

They have been used for stents to open blocked arteries.

[2]

03 A baby cup has been designed to change colour if hot liquids are poured into it.

[1]

Exam tip

Identify questions want you to name something.

Baby drinking cup

03.1 Identify the specific smart material required to give the baby drinking cup its specific functional property.

Specific smart material is: *Thermochromic pigment*

[2]

03.2 Explain why your chosen smart material is used in the manufacture of the baby drinking cup.

A thermochromic pigment is added to the base polymer so that the cup will change colour when filled with a hot drink. This will tell the parent if it is too hot for a child to safely drink.

[2]

Do you remember?

Modern materials, such as graphene, metal foams and titanium, have been made through the invention of new or improved processes.

Existing materials, such as coated metals, Liquid Crystal Displays (LCDs) and nanomaterials, have also been altered to perform a particular function.

You should revise modern and smart materials in more detail before looking at the questions on this page.

04 Titanium is a modern material.

04.1 Give **two** other examples of modern materials.

1. ....

2. ....

[2]

04.2 Explain **one** reason why titanium is used extensively in the aircraft industry.

....

....

[2]

05 Smart materials such as thermochromic pigments respond to a change in external stimulus. Thermochromic pigments can be used in baby drinking cups.

Explain **one** other application of thermochromic pigments.

....

....

[2]

Total

/ 6

☹ 😐 ☺

Answers

04.1 Graphene,[1] metal foam,[1] LCDs,[1] coated materials,[1] nanomaterials.[1]

04.2 Titanium has excellent strength to weight properties[1] which means that it is very strong for products such as wings or landing gear without adding too much excess weight.[1]

Titanium can be alloyed[1] which means its properties can be tailored to specific requirements for aircraft parts such as landing gear which need to be good in compression or wings that need to be light yet have some flexibility.[1]

05 Thermochromic pigments can be added to printing inks[1] which can be used in strip thermometers to show the body temperature of a sick person.[1]

Pigments can be mixed in with polymer granules for injection moulding[1] which means they can be used in products such as feeding spoons for babies to indicate if the food is too hot.[1] Novelty colour-changing goods, e.g. t-shirts / sunglasses.[1]

3.1.3 COMPOSITE MATERIALS AND TECHNICAL TEXTILES

Do you remember?

- A composite is a material made from at least two different materials.
- Technical textiles are manufactured for their functional performance.

You need to be familiar with how each material is made up to provide its unique properties. For example, Kevlar® fibres are arranged in layers, woven to form a strong net with an interlocking structure. This helps it resist bullets when used in body armour.

Microencapsulation of fabrics with medicines or anti-microbial coatings, for example, can be used to enhance their properties.

01 Name **one** specific composite material used in the manufacture of a prosthetic limb.

Carbonfibre reinforced plastic (CRF)

[1]

Do you remember?

The other composite material used in products is Glass Reinforced Plastic (GRP)

It is used to make products such as:

- Rigid pond liners
- Surf boards
- Canoes

Exam tip

Describe questions require you to set out the characteristics of something. You need to make an initial point, then expand it with further points for each additional mark.

02 Describe how conductive fibres can improve a textile-based product.

Conductive fibres allow electrical signals to pass through them. This means they can be used in clothing to connect components like LEDs together so clothes can light up. Clothing now exists where electrical devices such as a mobile phone in your pocket can be controlled by touching textile-based switches on gloves or jacket sleeves.

[3]

03 Explain **one** reason why police body armour is manufactured from Kevlar®.

Kevlar is puncture proof, therefore a knife or bullet is less likely to penetrate it offering greater protection to the person wearing it.

[2]

04 Give **two** ways in which technical textiles are used to help protect a firefighter.

1. ....

2. ....

[2]

05 Explain how Carbonfibre Reinforced Plastic is constructed to give it its special properties as a composite material.

....

....

....

....

[2]

06 GoreTex is breathable, yet waterproof.

06.1 Describe how GoreTex can be breathable yet waterproof.

....

....

....

....

....

....

[3]

06.2 Give **one** use of GoreTex fabric.

....

[1]

Total /8

Answers

04 Heat / fire proof clothing to protect from extreme heat / flames,[1] chemical splashes when dealing with toxic substances,[1] breathable fabrics to allow for perspiration,[1] to provide high visibility in areas where it may be dark / restricted visibility due to smoke in the air.[1]

05 It is woven[1] from single strands of carbon fibre into a flexible cloth or sheet.[1] These fibres have great tensile strength, but poor compressive strength. By combining with a thermosetting polymer resin, (brushing or rolling on) the cloth / sheet is no longer flexible once the polymer cures / sets.[1]

06.1 GoreTex pores are too small to let water from rain drops in,[1] keeping the wearer dry.[1] The pores are big enough to let sweat vapours / perspiration out,[1] keeping the wearer cooler[1] and drier.[1]

06.2 One from: Shoe uppers, jackets, outdoor sports clothing e.g. cycling / running / skiing / climbing.[1]

3.1.4 SYSTEMS APPROACH TO DESIGNING

01 Which **one** of the following components is an input?

  A A buzzer ⬚
  B A Light Dependent Resistor (LDR) ■
  C A motor ⬚
  D A speaker ⬚

[1]

> **Exam tip**
> When faced with a multiple choice question, try to work out what each of the answers mean one by one so that you can eliminate the wrong answers; for example, a buzzer, motor and speaker are all outputs so the answer must be B, the LDR.
>
> Temperature sensors, pressure sensors and switches are also input devices.

02 Name the flowchart symbol shown in **Figure 1**.

> **Exam tip**
> **Identify** questions want you to name something.

Figure 1

> **Do you remember?**
> There are different symbols for inputs, processes, decisions and outputs, and for starting or stopping a flowchart.
>
> **Decisions** can involve the use of programming microcontrollers as counters or timers.

Decision.

[1]

03 Give **two** applications of a buzzer.

1. *Doorbells*

2. *Alarms*

[2]

> **Do you remember?**
> An output component can make a sound, emit light, give off heat or create movement.
>
> *Which ones do you remember?*
> - *Buzzer*
> - *Light Emitting Diode (LED)*
> - *Lamp*
> - *Speaker*

04 What is the electrical component shown in **Figure 2**?

Figure 2

A A battery ⬭

B A buzzer ⬭

C A lamp ⬭

D A light-dependent resistor ⬭

[1]

05 Name the flowchart symbol shown in **Figure 3**.

Figure 3

....

[1]

06 Explain the operation of a light dependent resistor (LDR).

....

....

....

....

[2]

Total

/ 4

☹ 😐 ☺

Answers

04 B. A buzzer.[1]

05 Start or stop.[1]

06 An LDR senses changes in light levels[1] at which point its resistance goes up or down depending on how the light level changes.[1]

3.1.5

MECHANICAL DEVICES

DIFFERENT TYPES OF MOVEMENT AND LEVERS

01 Which **one** of the following definitions best describes a linear movement?

- **A** Movement in a straight line in one direction ●
- **B** Movement in a straight line forwards and backwards ○
- **C** Movement in a circular motion in one direction ○
- **D** Movement in a circular motion that swings forwards and backwards ○

[1]

Do you remember?

There are four different types of movement: linear, reciprocal, rotary and oscillation.

02 Which type of motion best describes the movement of a child on a swing?

Oscillation.

[1]

03 **Figure 1** shows a pair of scissors.

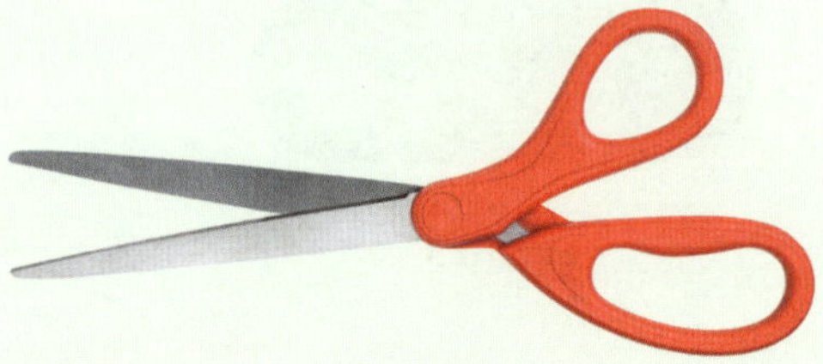

Figure 1

Do you remember?

There are **three** parts to a lever: the fulcrum, the load and the effort.

FLE123 is a way to remember which one is in the middle, e.g. the **F**ulcrum is in the middle for a Class **1** lever, **L**oad is in the middle for a Class **2** lever and **E**ffort is in the middle for a Class **3** lever.

Do you remember?

Levers have different classes or orders. The terms are interchangeable.

03.1 State what order of lever the scissors are.

First order

[1]

03.2 Calculate the Mechanical Advantage (MA) for the scissors shown in **Figure 1** if the Load is 100N and the Effort is 20N.

Use the formula $MA = \frac{\text{Load}}{\text{Effort}}$

MA = 100/20 = 5/1 or just MA = 5

[1]

Exam tip

A **calculate** question requires you to work out the value of something. It is always recommended to show ALL your working out.

04 Which **one** of the following types of motion best describes the action of the hands on a clock face?

A Linear ⬭

B Oscillation ⬭

C Reciprocation ⬭

D Rotary ⬭

[1]

05 **Figure 2** shows a stapler.

Figure 2

05.1 State what order or class of lever the stapler is.

....

[1]

05.2 Calculate the Mechanical Advantage (MA) for the stapler shown in **Figure 2** if the Load is 25N and the Effort is 50N.

Use the formula $MA = \frac{Load}{Effort}$

....

[1]

05.3 Explain **one** reason why the effort must be larger than the load for the stapler shown in **Figure 2**.

....

....

[2]

Total / 5

Answers

04 D. Rotary.[1]

05.1 Third order / class 3.[1]

05.2 MA = Load/Effort = 25/50 = 0.5[1]

05.3 The load is further away from the fulcrum than the effort[1] *which means a bigger effort is required to be able to carry out the work required at the point of the load.*[1]

3.1.5

MECHANICAL DEVICES

LINKAGES AND ROTARY SYSTEMS

01 State which type of linkage would be used to change the direction of an input motion through 90°.

Bell crank.

[1]

02 Cams are used to convert rotary motion into different movements.

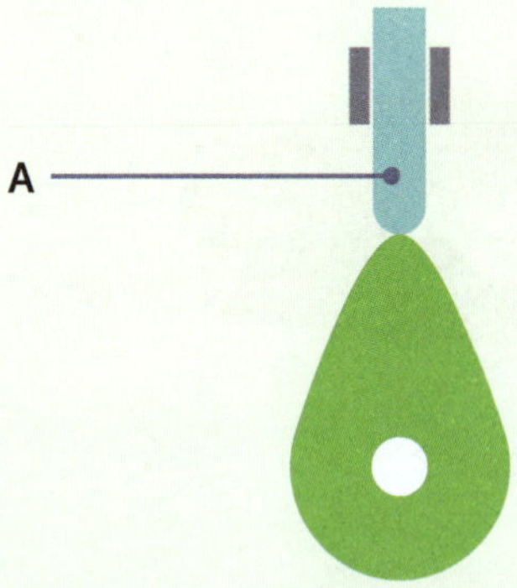

Figure 1

Figure 1 shows a cam and a component labelled **A**.
Give the name of the component labelled A in **Figure 1**.

Follower.

[1]

03 **Figure 2** shows a simple gear train.

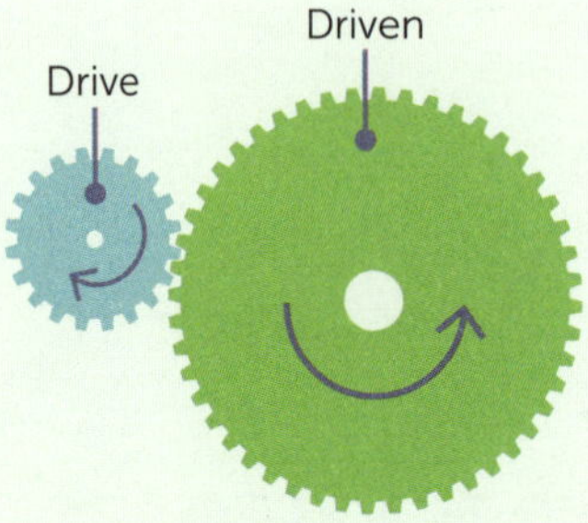

Figure 2

Calculate the velocity ratio (VR), if the drive gear has 20 teeth and the driven gear has 48 teeth.

Use the formula $VR = \frac{\text{number of teeth on driven gear}}{\text{number of teeth on drive gear}}$

$VR = 48 \div 20 = 2.4$

[2]

04 Explain **one** reason why toothed belts are used with toothed pulleys rather than V belts.

A toothed belt provides a physical connection with a toothed pulley and is therefore much less likely to slip when transferring rotational forces from one shaft to another.

[2]

Do you remember?

A push/pull mechanism will maintain the direction of movement.

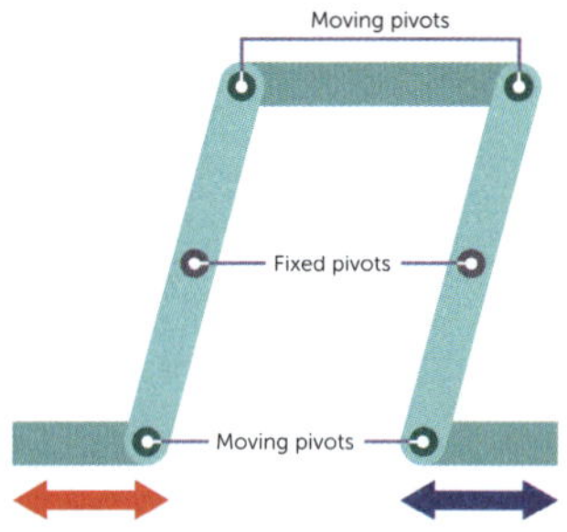

Do you remember?

There are **four** main types of CAM:

- Circular or eccentric
- Pear
- Snail
- Heart shaped

Exam tip

Always show your working to ensure that even if your answer is wrong, that you get marks for showing the correct method in working out your answer.

05 The ironing board in **Figure 3** uses a linkage mechanism in its design.

Explain how the linkage helps in the function of the ironing board for the user.

Figure 3

....

....

....

[3]

06 Study **Figure 4** of a pulley and belt system.

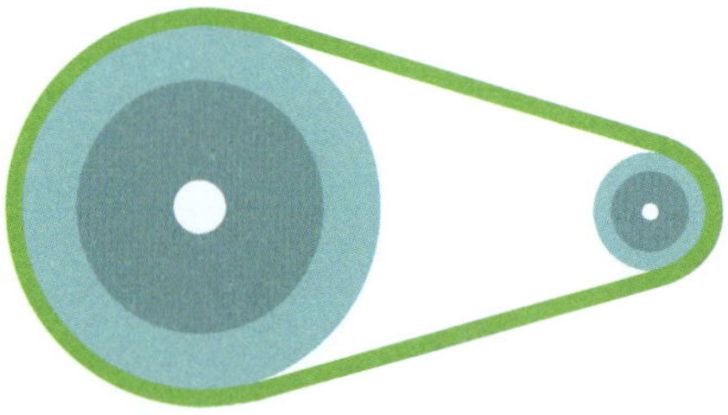

Figure 4

Left Pulley	Right Pulley
Diameter 210mm	Diameter 70mm

The pulley on the left rotates at 900 revolutions per minute (rpm).
Calculate how many revolutions per minute (rpm) the pulley on the right will turn.

....

....

....

[3]

Total

/ 6

☹ 😐 ☺

Answers

05 The mechanism allows the board to collapse / fold flat[1] which this makes it easier to store away in a smaller space[1] when not in use.[1] The mechanism will also allow for the board to be adjustable to different heights[1] for different height people[1] to fit better ergonomically.[1]

06

1 mark	210 / 70 = 3
1 mark	900 x 3
1 mark	2700 rpm

3.1.6.1

MATERIALS AND THEIR WORKING PROPERTIES

PAPERS AND BOARDS

Exam tip

In Section A of the exam paper, you need to know a little bit about all material groups as you could have to answer short questions on any of them.

The following pages contain example questions from each material area.

01 Name **two** specific types of paper.

1. *Bleed proof paper*

2. *Cartridge paper*

[2]

Do you remember?

You could also have named grid, layout, or tracing paper.

Do you remember?

There are **five** material groups you need to know about:

- Papers and boards
- Natural and manufactured timbers
- Metals and alloys
- Polymers
- Textiles

02 Explain how papers and boards are classified.

Papers usually weigh less than boards. A paper is classified in grams per square metre (gsm) and usually weighs less than 200 gsm. Boards can be classified in gsm, but can also be classified by their thickness in microns e.g. 1000 microns = 1 mm.

[3]

03 What is the specific name of the material shown in **Figure 1**?

Figure 1

The material shown is: *Corrugated cardboard.*

[1]

04 Explain **one** reason why foil lined board is used in takeaway containers.

The foil reflects heat back into the container to stop the food from going cold too quickly.

[2]

Do you remember?

The foil is laminated onto the card. The card stiffens and supports the foil and provides some degree of insulation. The foil also acts as a barrier to stop the card going soggy and as an antimicrobial protection layer.

05 Name **two** specific paper-based boards.

1. ....

2. ....

[2]

06 Name a specific suitable type of board for making an architectural model and give **one detailed** reason for your choice.

Board name: ....

Reason for choice: ....

....

....

....

[3]

07 Give **one** example of use for duplex board.

....

....

[1]

08 Give **one** advantage and **one** disadvantage of using corrugated cardboard for packaging.

Advantage: ....

....

Disadvantage: ....

....

[2]

Total / 8

Answers

05 Boards: Corrugated, duplex, foil lined, foam core, solid white. One mark for each.[1]

06 Board name = Foam core board.[1]

Reason(s) = Lightweight and rigid.[1]

A thick board which is very rigid in all directions[1] so can support a model under its own weight.[1]

Available in a variety of colours highly suited to model making[1]

Very smooth surface and finish[1] to which other detail can be added to make a model more realistic e.g., brick work.[1]

07 Used on a food containers[1] e.g. a box to hold cakes purchased in a bakery.[1]

08 Advantages: good protection of contents / low cost / printable / rigid / stackable.[1]

Disadvantages: loses strength when wet, less rigid along flutes..[1]

3.1.6.1

MATERIALS AND THEIR WORKING PROPERTIES

NATURAL AND MANUFACTURED TIMBERS

01 Name **two** manufactured timbers.

MDF, chipboard.

[2]

Do you remember?

Manufactured timbers are made from wood fibres, chips, strips, batons, or thin sheets of wood stuck together with adhesives.

02 Describe how a hardwood tree and a softwood tree are likely to differ in appearance when growing.

Hardwood trees tend to lose their leaves in autumn and have larger leaves. Softwood trees usually have needles instead of leaves and are often triangular in shape e.g. Christmas tree shape.

[3]

03 What is the specific name of the material shown in **Figure 1**?

Figure 1

The material shown is: *Plywood*

[1]

04 Give **one** reason why beech is a suitable wood to make a traditional child's toy.

Beech is close grained and finishes well. It also does not splinter easily so it is less likely to harm a child if they chew it.

[1]

Do you remember?

You need to be aware of the following types of timber:
Hardwoods: Ash, beech, mahogany, oak and balsa.
Softwoods: Larch, pine and spruce.

05 Name **two** specific manufactured timbers.

1. ....

2. ....

[2]

06 Name a specific suitable manufactured timber for making flat pack furniture and give **one detailed** reason for your choice.

Manufactured timber name: ....

Reason for choice: ....

....

....

....

[3]

07 Explain **one** property that makes ash a good material choice for the hammer shaft shown in **Figure 2**.

Figure 2

....

....

....

....

[2]

Total /7

Answers

05 Any one from plywood, chipboard, laminboard, blockboard, OSB (Oriented Stand Board), MDF.[1]

06 Timber name = MDF (Medium Density Fibreboard) / HDF / laminated chipboard / plywood.[1]
Reason(s) = Available in large flat sheets.[1] of a constant thickness[1] making it easier for a manufacturer to produce precision engineered furniture[1] on a mass produced scale.[1]
MDF has a smooth finish[1] and it does not have any knots[1] or surface defects[1] that may reduce the quality of the product over time.[1]

07 Ash is a shock resistant wood[1] which withstands sudden impacts well.[1] It is a springy,[1] flexible[1] wood.

3.1.6.1

MATERIALS AND THEIR WORKING PROPERTIES

METALS AND ALLOYS

01 Explain why metals are alloyed.

Metals and other elements e.g. carbon are mixed together to produce a new metal with better or enhanced properties so that it works more successfully in a design situation.

[2]

What is an alloy?

An alloy is a mixture of two or more metals or other elements. These include brass, stainless steel and high-speed steel.

02 Name **two** non-ferrous metals.

1. *Tin.*
2. *Copper.*

[2]

Do you remember?

Non-ferrous metals do not contain any iron (ferrite).

03 Describe a school workshop test you could use to tell if a metal was ferrous or non-ferrous.

Use a magnet. If the magnet sticks to the metal, it is ferrous because the magnet is attracted to the iron within it.

[2]

04 Label each of the metal products in **Figure 1** as ferrous or non-ferrous.

[2]

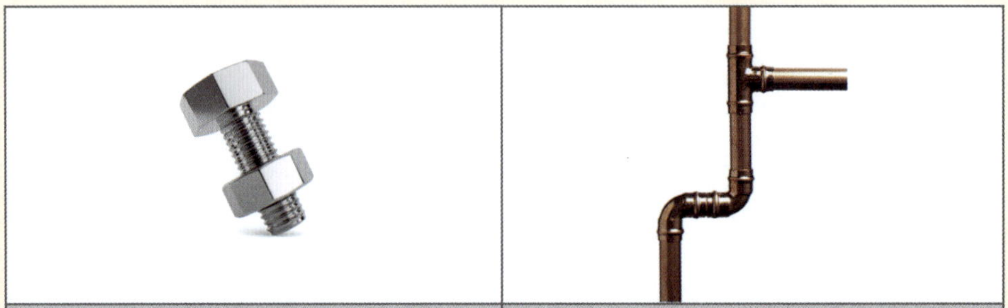

Mild steel nut and bolt	Copper plumbing pipe
Ferrous	*Non-ferrous*

Figure 1

Do you remember?

Low and high carbon steel are considered ferrous metals.

Stainless steel and high-speed (tool) steel are ferrous alloys.

05 Which of the materials below is a ferrous metal?

A Aluminium ⬭

B Brass ⬭

C Steel ⬭

D Zinc ⬭

[1]

06 Name **two** specific metal alloys.

1. ....

2. ....

[2]

07 Name a specific ferrous metal suitable for making a child's climbing frame and give **one detailed** reason for your choice.

Suitable ferrous metal: ....

Reason for choice: ....

....

....

....

[3]

Total

/ 6

☹ 😐 ☺

Answers

05 C. Steel.[1]

06 Alloys: Brass,[1] high speed steel,[1] stainless steel.[1]

07 Suitable ferrous metal = Steel,[1] mild steel.[1]

Reason(s) = Can be purchased in tube stock form[1] which is good for bending[1] the different shaped parts required in a climbing frame.

Steel can be painted or powder coated in bright colours[1] to make it more attractive to children.[1]

3.1.6.1

MATERIALS AND THEIR WORKING PROPERTIES

POLYMERS

01 Define what is meant by thermoforming polymer.

A thermoforming polymer is one that becomes soft when heated and can then be moulded and shaped. Once cooled, thermoforming polymers become rigid again. If heated a second time they soften again and can take on a new or different shape.

[2]

Do you remember?

Thermoforming polymers are sometimes called thermoplastics. They include acrylic (PMMA), high impact polystyrene (HIPS), high density polyethylene (HDPE), polypropylene (PP), polyvinyl chloride (PVC) and polyethylene terephthalate (PET).

02 Name **two** thermosetting polymers.

1. *Epoxy Resin (ER)*
2. *Melamine Formaldehyde (MF)*

[2]

Do you remember?

You may have seen epoxy resin widely used as an adhesive. It comes in two tubes (a resin and a hardener). You mix equal amounts together. It's really good at joining dissimilar materials.

Other thermosets include phenol formaldehyde (PF), polyester resin (PR), and urea-formaldehyde (UF).

03 Which of the polymers below is a thermoforming polymer?

A Acrylic [filled]
B Epoxy resin [ ]
C Polyester resin [ ]
D Urea formaldehyde [ ]

[1]

04 Explain why polymer cups and plates that go in a dishwasher should be made from thermosetting polymers.

Dishwashers use very hot water to get the cups and plates clean. The temperature can be too great for thermoforming polymers so cups and plates made from the wrong polymer might start to soften, change shape, and distort.

[2]

Exam tip

The exam paper may give you a scenario that you should be familiar with to find out what you know about a topic. You should include the context in your response with a point and a reason.

05 Describe how thermoforming polymers and thermosetting polymers are different.

....

....

....

....

....

[3]

06 Which of the polymers below is a thermoforming polymer?

A Epoxy resin ☐

B Phenol formaldehyde ☐

C Polypropylene ☐

D Urea formaldehyde ☐

[1]

07 Name a specific thermosetting polymer suitable for making a kitchen work surface and give **one detailed** reason for your choice.

Suitable thermosetting polymer: ....

Reason for choice: ....

....

....

....

[3]

Total /7

Answers

05 Points include:

- *A thermoforming polymer is one that becomes soft when heated and can be moulded and shaped.*
- *Once cooled thermoforming polymers become rigid again.*
- *If heated a second time they soften again and can take on a new or different shape.*
- *Thermosetting polymers do not change shape with heat once set. They undergo a chemical change during manufacture which cannot be reversed by re heating.*
- *Thermosetting polymers have more crosslinks preventing them from softening.*
- *Thermosets char, instead of burning, making them safer for electrical insulation.*

06 C. Polypropylene.[1]

07 Suitable thermosetting polymer: Melamine formaldehyde,[1] Formica.[1]
Reason(s):

- *A waterproof and heat resistant surface (more resistant to damage by hot pans) that can be bonded to MDF.*
- *Hard wearing in a kitchen environment e.g. resists most scratching.*
- *Ease to wipe down and sanitise.*
- *Can be printed or coloured for varied aesthetics.*

MATERIALS AND THEIR WORKING PROPERTIES
3.1.6.1 TEXTILES

01 Which of the materials below is a naturally occurring fibre?

- A Silk ●
- B Lycra ○
- C Nylon ○
- D Polyester ○

[1]

> **Do you remember?**
>
> Natural fibres come from plants and animals. Synthetic fibres usually come from finite resources such as oil. You need to know the properties of a range of natural and synthetic fibres.

02 Explain where synthetic fibres come from.

Synthetic fibres cannot be grown from plants or animals.

They come out of the ground as oil, which is another use of fossil fuels.

[2]

> **Do you remember?**
>
> Fibres can also be woven together. Non-woven fabrics may be bonded together or matted as felt.

03 Give **one** advantage and **one** disadvantage of knitted clothing.

Advantage: *Can make stretchy clothing to fit your shape better.*

Disadvantage: *Can shrink when you put it in the wash at the wrong temperature.*

[2]

> **Exam tip**
>
> Think about your experience of knitted clothing. Was it warm? Did it itch? Did it lose its shape after a few washes?

04 Give **one** specific example of a blended or mixed fibre.

Polycotton. (Cotton and polyester.)

[1]

05 Identify the natural fibre harvested form the source shown in **Figure 1**.

Figure 1

A Cotton ⬭

B Leather ⬭

C Silk ⬭

D Wool ⬭

[1]

06 Explain why wool is a good material choice for clothing.
Give **one** example of use in your answer .

....

....

....

....

[3]

07 Name a specific synthetic fibre used in sportswear and give **one detailed** reason for your choice.

Suitable synthetic fibre: ....

Reason for choice: ....

....

....

....

[3]

Total /7

Answers

05 *A. Cotton.*[1]

06 *Wool is a good insulator so it can keep you warm on cold days.*[1] *Wool can be dyed to change its colour to suit different tastes.*[1] *Wool is a sustainable material, so it does not use up the earth's finite resources.*[1] *Examples are jumpers*[1] *and gloves.*[1]

07 *Suitable synthetic fibre = Polyamide,*[1] *Nylon,*[1] *Elastane,*[1] *Lycra*[1]
Reason(s):
Polyamide/Nylon = a lightweight and hard-wearing material. Washes well over time. Non-absorbent and crease resistant.
Elastane/Lycra = smooth to touch. Very strong in use. Machine washable and crease resistant. Quick drying for swimming costumes. Very elastic and holds its shape.

3.1.6.2 MATERIAL PROPERTIES

01 Which **one** of the following is a physical property?

A Density ⬬
B Malleability ○
C Toughness ○
D Strength ○

Malleability
How a material bends or can be shaped.

Strength
How a material resists force without breaking.

[1]

02 Describe why children's toys need to be made from tough and durable materials.

Children can be rough when playing. Toys can get dropped and brittle parts may snap off.

Toys that are not tough may break easily and that would mean money is wasted on a poor-quality toy.

The child will also get upset that they can no longer play with their toy.

Children often chew their toys, so for safety reasons no one wants bits to break off that can be swallowed.

[2]

Exam tip

Describe questions require you to talk about the characteristics and features of something.

03 **Figure 1** shows a lifejacket.

03.1 Name the physical property required in the life jacket below for it to work.

Exam tip

It is a good idea to clarify your answer, if possible, i.e., low density

Figure 1

Density / low density

[1]

Do you remember?

Material properties are more than just their physical appearance and form e.g., colour, conductivity, absorbency etc.

Material properties require you to know about how materials behave when being used in products and the forces and stresses they must work with.

See physical and working properties on **page 36**.

03.2 State why the physical property named in **03.1** is so important for the life jacket to work.

The life jacket needs to float and be buoyant so that a person in the water does not sink and drown. The main material needs to be less dense than water.

[1]

Exam tip

Try to add detail to your answer to make sure you get all available marks. This answer has two good points of clarification explaining why buoyancy is important and that the life jacket needs to use a material less dense than water.

04 Which of the following is a working property?

A Absorbency ☐

B Density ☐

C Ductility ☐

D Fusibility ☐

[1]

05 **Figure 2** shows copper tracks on a Printed Circuit Board (PCB).

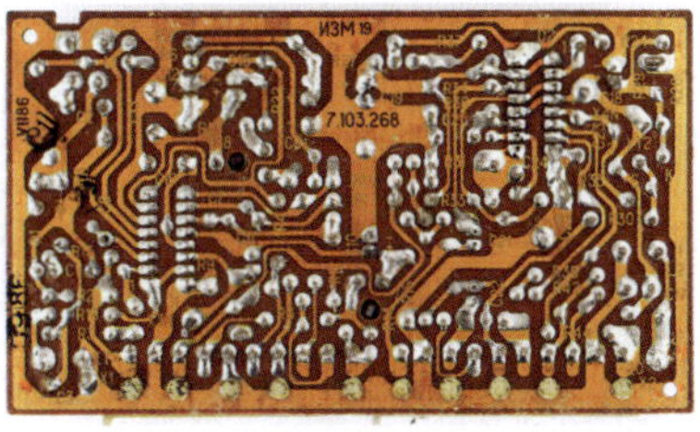

Figure 2

05.1 Name the physical property needed in the copper tracks.

Physical property: ....

[2]

05.2 Explain why the physical property named in **05.1** is so important for the PCB to work.

....

....

....

[2]

06 Explain why it is important for sportswear to be absorbent.

....

....

....

....

[3]

Total / 8

☹ 😐 ☺

Answers

04 *C. Ductility.*[1] The ability of a material to be stretched, drawn or pulled without breaking.

05.1 *Electrical conductivity.*[2] *Both words gain two marks. Conductivity only gets one mark.*

05.2 *The copper tracks need to have good electrical conductivity so the electrical current can flow from one component to another*[1] *and make the circuit work.*[1] *Copper has low resistance.*[1]

06 *When exercising, athletes perspire*[1] *and get hot.*[1] *By having sportswear that is absorbent, sweat is drawn away from the body,*[1] *making it more comfortable for the athlete when exercising.*[1] *When sweat is drawn away from the body, it is called wicking which is a desirable property in sportswear,*[1] *to keep the athlete cool.*[1]

PHYSICAL AND WORKING PROPERTIES

It is important to know the physical and working properties of a range of materials.

Physical properties

The physical properties of any material can be measured in their natural state.

Absorbency

The ability of a material to soak up or draw in heat, light or moisture.

Example: Cotton is more absorbent than acrylic.

Thermal conductivity

The measure of a material's ability to transfer heat.

Example: Copper is an excellent conductor of heat.

Electrical conductivity

The measure at which a material can transport electricity.

Example: Copper is a good conductor of electricity. Insulators such as plastic or rubber do not conduct electricity.

Density

The mass, per unit volume of any material. How solid is a material.

Example: Polystyrene has a low density, suitable for packaging. Lead has high density, suitable for weights.

Fusibility

The ability of a material to be converted from a solid to a fluid state by heat and combined with another material.

Example: Fusibility is a useful for metals and polymers to aid casting and welding.

Working properties

Working properties describe how a material responds when it is manipulated or worked.

Ductility

The ability of a material to be stretched, drawn or pulled without breaking.

Example: Copper is ductile so can be drawn out to make wire.

Elasticity

The ability to return to its original shape after stretching or compression.

Example: Lycra is used for sportswear to provide freedom of movement.

Hardness

The ability to withstand impact, wear, abrasion and indentation.

Example: Tungsten is hard, used for knives, drills and saws.

Strength

The ability to withstand a force such as pressure, compression, tension or shear.

Example: May be strong in one force and not another. Concrete is strong under compression, but not tension.

Malleability

The ability to be bent and shaped without cracking or splitting.

Example: Gold, copper, silver and lead can all be easily hammered into shape.

Toughness

The ability to absorb shock without fracturing.

Example: Kevlar® body armour absorbs impact.

SECTION B

3.2 SPECIALIST TECHNICAL PRINCIPLES

Information

At least 15% of the exam will assess maths and at least 10% will assess science.

There are 100 marks in total. 20 marks for Section A, 30 for Section B and 50 for Section C.

All questions are mandatory.

All dimensions are in millimetres.

!

You will need:
A black pen (and some spares)

You may also use:
An HB pencil, ruler and other normal writing and drawing instruments
A calculator
A protractor

Exam tip

In Section B of the exam paper, you will have to answer some questions in relation to **at least one** material area that you have specialised in and studied in more depth and detail in class.

For each question, you may choose the material area you feel most comfortable writing about to demonstrate your knowledge, even if it isn't your specialist area.

3.2.1

SELECTION OF MATERIALS OR COMPONENTS

FUNCTIONALITY, AESTHETICS, BULK BUYING, SOCIAL AND CULTURAL FACTORS

01 Outline the main reasons for a manufacturer to bulk buy materials and components. **[3]**

When a manufacturer bulk buys, they can purchase the materials or components they need for a cheaper price. They should be able to get the best deals available for the lowest price. This means they can manufacture a product for a lower price meaning the customer can get a better deal. It also makes the company more competitive. By bulk buying, a manufacturer is less likely to run out of essential materials and components causing production to stop or slow whilst waiting for new deliveries.

Exam tip

Outline questions requires you to set out the main characteristic and features of something.

- Where 3 marks are available, the examiner is looking for **at least two points** to be made.
- **At least one needs to be clarified in detail.**

Do you remember?

Aesthetics are about appearance and beauty. Both concepts are subjective to individuals and are referred to as personal taste.

02 Give **one** detailed reason why **each** aesthetic point below is an important consideration in selecting materials and components for use. **[2 x 2]**

Appearance of surface finish: *By choosing a smooth finish, a manufacturer may save time in production not having to sand and smooth the surface of a material. Components may be purchased with a finish already applied to stop them corroding, decaying, or fading to keep the product looking new.* **[2]**

Colour: *Selecting materials or components of a particular colour means they match or complement a colour scheme or a range of other products and accessories. Different colour options also allow customers to make a personal choice.* **[2]**

03 What is meant by 'functionality' when considering material selection? **[2]**

Functionality takes into consideration if a material selected for use is fit for purpose and whether it will work properly if or when used in the construction of a product.

Exam tip

What questions require you to give the correct information.

04 A mechanical child's toy is manufactured using 6 springs. The springs are sold in bulk units of 100. How many bulk units of 100 would need to be purchased to make 300 toys? **[2]**

How many springs are needed in total = 300 x 6 = 1800

How many bulk units of 100 are needed = 18 bulk units

05 Outline the main reasons why the following **two** factors need to be considered when selecting materials and components for use.

Cultural: ....

....

....

Social: ....

....

....

[2 × 2]

06 During the manufacture of a coat, 4 buttons and 1 spare button are required.

06.1 Calculate how many buttons are required to make 2500 coats.

....

....

....

[2]

06.2 Each button costs 10p.

The manufacturer is given a 20% discount for bulk buying.

What will be the total cost of the buttons to make 2500 coats?

Give your answer in pounds.

....

....

....

[3]

Total

/ 9

☹ 😐 ☺

Answers

05 Cultural: You have to be careful that when sourcing and using materials you do not offend a community or group of people[1] Some people have beliefs that mean certain colours[1] and materials cannot be used.[1]

Social: You also need to make sure that by extracting materials you do not impact negatively on a community[1] and where they live.[1] This can include things like deforestation[1] to harvest timber for wood and paper products.[1]

06.1 5 buttons per coat.[1] 2500 × 5 buttons to make all coats = 12,500 buttons.[1]

06.2 12,500 × 10p = 125,000p ***or*** *12,500 × £0.10 = £1250[1] 125,000 / 100 × 80[1] = 100,000p* ***or*** *1250 / 100 × 80[1]* ***or*** *1250 × 0.8[1] = £1000[1] (Remember to show the units: £.)*

Exam tip

At least 15% of the exam will assess maths skills. Always show your working out and tell the examiner what you are doing as you might get some method marks even if your final answer is incorrect.

3.2.1

SELECTION OF MATERIALS OR COMPONENTS

ENVIRONMENTAL, AVAILABILITY AND ETHICAL FACTORS

01 Explain why availability of materials is important to a manufacturer of a continuously produced product.

Give an example in your answer. **[3]**

When a product is in continuous demand it could be because it is a simple component used in the assembly of a more complicated product. If materials or components become harder to obtain, production of products such as cars and mobile phones may have to slow or stop. This happened in the pandemic with the production of integrated circuits used in lots of electronic goods.

> **Exam tip**
>
> Look how this answer has a clear example as required and is then clarified with an additional example.

02 Define the **two** terms below.

> **Exam tip**
>
> **Define** means give a specific meaning.

Recyclable: *Where waste materials are broken down by shredding, chopping, and grinding into new usable materials.* **[2]**

Reuse: *This is where a product or item is reused by possibly refilling it e.g. a printer cartridge or by using the item for a new purpose e.g. car tyres in swings in a playground.* **[2]**

[2 × 2]

> **Upcycling**
>
> **Upcycling** is a new term closely linked to reuse.
>
> Upcycling is all about reusing product that are at the end of their design life and creating a new useful product of value.

03 **Figure 1** shows a logo.

Identify and name the logo.

FSC
www.fsc.org

Figure 1

This logo is for: *Forest Stewardship Council.*

[1]

04 What is the meaning of the FSC logo when found on raw materials and components?

....

....

....

....

[2]

05 Give **one** specific example where a lack of material or component availability has impacted the manufacture of products.

....

....

[1]

06 Define the term 'upcycling'.

....

....

....

[2]

Total

/ 5

Answers

04 The FSC logo is found on timbers and papers sourced from ethical sources.[1] It means the materials were responsibly sourced from sustainable forests.[1] The sustainable management of forests means that new trees are planted to replace those that are chopped down to make timber-based products.[1]

05 The (Evergreen) container ship, carrying supplies and parts became stuck in the Suez canal in 2021.[1]
The pandemic resulted in a transistor / component shortage for new car manufacture.[1]
War and conflict e.g. Russia / Ukraine, impacted oil production and production of polymers / rubber e.g., car tyres.[1]

06 Reusing a product that has already lived a life and can then be turned into a new product with a different use[1] e.g., car tyres used to make plant pots and safety surfaces.[1]
Upcycling is where potential rubbish is repurposed[1] into a useful product.[1]

3.2.2 FORCES AND STRESSES

*You should have knowledge and understanding of forces and stresses for at least **one** material category.*

01 What force does the symbol in **Figure 1** show? **[1]**

Figure 1

The force shown is: *Shear*

> **Do you remember?**
>
> You also need to know about:
> - Tension
> - Compression
> - Bending
> - Torsion

02 Describe **one** way in which a material of your choice can be reinforced to improve its resistance to forces and stresses.
Give a specific example in your answer.

A shirt collar and cuffs can be stiffened to make them more rigid and keep their shape better for wear and use. This technique is called fabric interfacing. Other places on clothing where interfacing can be found are buttonholes, so it is easy to guide a button through.

Timbers can be laminated together in layers with the grain running in alternate directions at 90 degrees to each other to create plywood. This creates a large flat, stable board.

Concrete can be reinforced by adding steel bars. Concrete is good in compression but poor in tension. By adding steel bar reinforcement, you combine the best properties of both materials.

Polymers and rubber, e.g. car tyres can be reinforced by including webbing and steel belts into the layers of the tyre to provide additional strength and resistance against punctures and kerb damage. Polymer tape may be reinforced with thread to create duct tape.

Board can be reinforced by laminating paper or foil onto the surfaces or by creating corrugations for additional stability and strength perpendicular to the corrugations.

[4]

> **Exam tip**
>
> Make sure you give a clear example in your answer if one is asked for.

> **Do you remember?**
>
> You only need to know about one specific material area in section B. Answers are provided here as an example for all material areas.
>
> Other ways of reinforcing more suited to other materials are:
> - Lamination
> - Bending
> - Folding
> - Webbing

03 What force do the arrows show is acting on the spring in **Figure 2**?

Figure 2

The force shown is: ....

[1]

04 Identify and describe forces acting upon the crane in **Figure 3** below.

Figure 3

....

....

....

....

....

....

[4]

Total

/ 5

☹ 😐 ☺

Answers

03 Compression / compressive.[1]

04 Questions usually with four or more marks often use band descriptors to arrive at a best fit mark:

3–4 marks	Two or more specific forces identified **and** described in correct locations on the crane.
1–2 marks	One or two specific forces identified **and/or** described in correct locations on the crane.
0 marks	No attempt or nothing worthy of credit.

A typical response for the top band of marks would be:

The cables lifting the container are held in tension. They could also be in torsion if the cables are twisting in the wind. The tyres/feet of the crane are in compression with the weight of the crane acting upon them. The hydraulic ram is in compression with the weight of the crane and container acting upon it. The arm of the crane has to resist bending forces being applied as the container is lifted/lowered.

3.2.3 ECOLOGICAL AND SOCIAL FOOTPRINT

Exam tip

Don't forget to make sure you focus on key words and do a quick mini plan to help you arrange your answer as this question is for 8 marks.

01 Consumers are being encouraged by manufactures and wider society to recycle, re-use and repair. Analyse and evaluate the issues a consumer will consider in buying and using products they need and want. Give examples in your answer.

Exam tip

Analyse questions require you to set out the main characteristics and features of a context given in the question.

Evaluate questions require you to offer your own opinion and make judgements e.g., good and bad points about a given context.

Do you remember?

In section A of the exam paper, you have to know about sustainability and the environment. You can use your knowledge and understanding of these topics here too.

The six Rs should be considered in related responses: reduce, refuse, re-use, repair, recycle and rethink.

Society increasingly encourages consumers to recycle products at the end of their life and to recycle the packaging they came in to save resources, especially finite resources. Consumers are continually reminded that recycling saves energy, meaning fossil fuels do not need to be burned to generate energy for transporting new raw materials to a factory for processing into stock forms.

Consumers can be told by some manufactures how some products can be reused e.g., by refilling a kitchen surface spray bottle from a refill pouch. A refill pouch only uses polymers whereas the trigger spray bottle uses different materials such as steel to make the spring inside the trigger. These are also difficult to separate and recycle when the bottle is finished. Often it is still working perfectly well and not at the end of its life.

Customers are increasingly encouraged to repair items e.g. clothing or repairing a phone screen by buying a replacement one. This is not only better for the environment, but is more economical than buying a replacement phone.

[8]

Analyse Evaluate Example

02 Poorly designed products made from rare or finite resources are damaging the ecology of our planet.

Analyse and evaluate specific ways this damage is occurring and what measures can be taken to reduce ecological damage.

Give examples in your answer.

....

....

....

....

....

....

....

....

....

....

....

....

....

....

....

....

....

....

....

....

....

....

[8]

Total

/ 8

☹ 😐 ☺

Answers

See extended response answer on ***page 46***

ANSWERS

02 Some questions, usually with four or more marks, use band descriptors to arrive at a best fit mark:

7–8 marks	A very detailed analysis and evaluation of a range of ecological factors leading to damage of the planet. Several examples used to support an answer.
5–6 marks	A detailed analysis and evaluation of some ecological factors leading to damage of the planet. At least one example used to support an answer.
3–4 marks	A basic analysis and/or evaluation of some ecological factors leading to damage of the planet. Possible examples used to support an answer.
1–2 marks	One or two ecological factors identified. No examples given.
0 marks	No attempt or nothing worthy of credit.

Credit will be given to valid responses which are not included below. Possible responses could make reference to:

Material extraction

Deforestation

Damage	Measures to reduce impact
Removal of trees to make timber-based products involves chopping down trees, leading to soil erosion and desertification. Forests are cleared to expose the ground for raw material extraction e.g., metals and ores.	Sustainable replanting of trees i.e., replant at least one tree for every one felled. Reduce the need for raw material extraction by recycling, reusing or reducing.

Mining

Damage	Measures to reduce impact
Open cast mining and quarrying involves the removal of topsoil. Contamination of local environment.	Creation of nature reserves and land reclamation for environmental and leisure uses e.g., water sports. Ensure correct procedures are followed for chemicals or leachate.

Drilling

Damage	Measures to reduce impact
Pollution and destruction of ecosystems e.g., chemicals pumped into the ground when fracking.	Refuse to continue with this form of energy production.

Farming

Damage	Measures to reduce impact
Land clearance for grazing. Methane (CH_4) emissions. Excessive water consumption for cotton crops and livestock.	Use of upcycled and recycled fabrics for clothing. Use of recycled polymers to make clothing. Greater range of plant-based foods.

Transportation

Product miles

Damage	Measures to reduce impact
Fuels and emissions / pollution created by transporting raw materials and products throughout their lifecycle.	Local sourcing of materials. Manufacture of products in the country of sale.

Pollution

Atmospheric pollution

Damage	Measures to reduce impact
Burning of fossil fuels releasing CO_2 and SO_2 leading to global warming, melting of ice caps, and breathing problems for the elderly and ill.	Move away from fossil fuels and increase development of green energy e.g., solar, wind and hydro. Development of carbon capture schemes to lock liquified CO_2 into disused oil fields deep under the sea.

Oceanic pollution

Damage	Measures to reduce impact
Dumping of chemicals e.g., mercury and plastics, into the oceans, destroying habitats, affecting marine life and entering the food chain.	Ocean clean up systems e.g., the ships Forrest and Jenny trawling for polymers in the oceans. Increased recycling rates.

Carbon footprint

Carbon production in the design and manufacture of a product

Damage	Measures to reduce impact
Carbon produced by machinery and equipment extracting, refining, and processing materials. Carbon generated by products using fossil fuels to work or using energy created from fossil fuels.	Recycle and reuse materials to significantly reduce the need for raw material extraction e.g., oil to make new plastics. Use green energy and avoid leaving electrical devices turned on or on standby.

3.2.4

SOURCES AND ORIGINS

PAPERS AND BOARDS

Note:

In Section B of the exam paper, you may be asked a question with a range of suitable responses according to the specific material area that you have studied. Your responses to any question in this section can be from any material area. You may have studied more than one. The next set of pages consider what a possible response from each specialist material area could look like.

You should have knowledge and understanding of sources and origins for **at least one** material category.

01 **Table 1** shows a range of materials.

Choose **one** of the materials in the table below:

Cartridge paper	Pine	Steel	PVC	Denim

Table 1

My chosen material is: *Cartridge paper.*

Exam tip

Choose questions require you to make a choice. As this is a material question, you should choose the option that best fits the main material area you have studied for the course.

01.1 Name a specific source of your chosen material.

Wood pulp. **[1]**

Exam tip

Make sure that you do what the question says and use notes and sketches in your answer for a possible maximum mark.

01.2 In the box below, use notes and sketches to explain how your chosen material is converted from its primary source into a usable form.

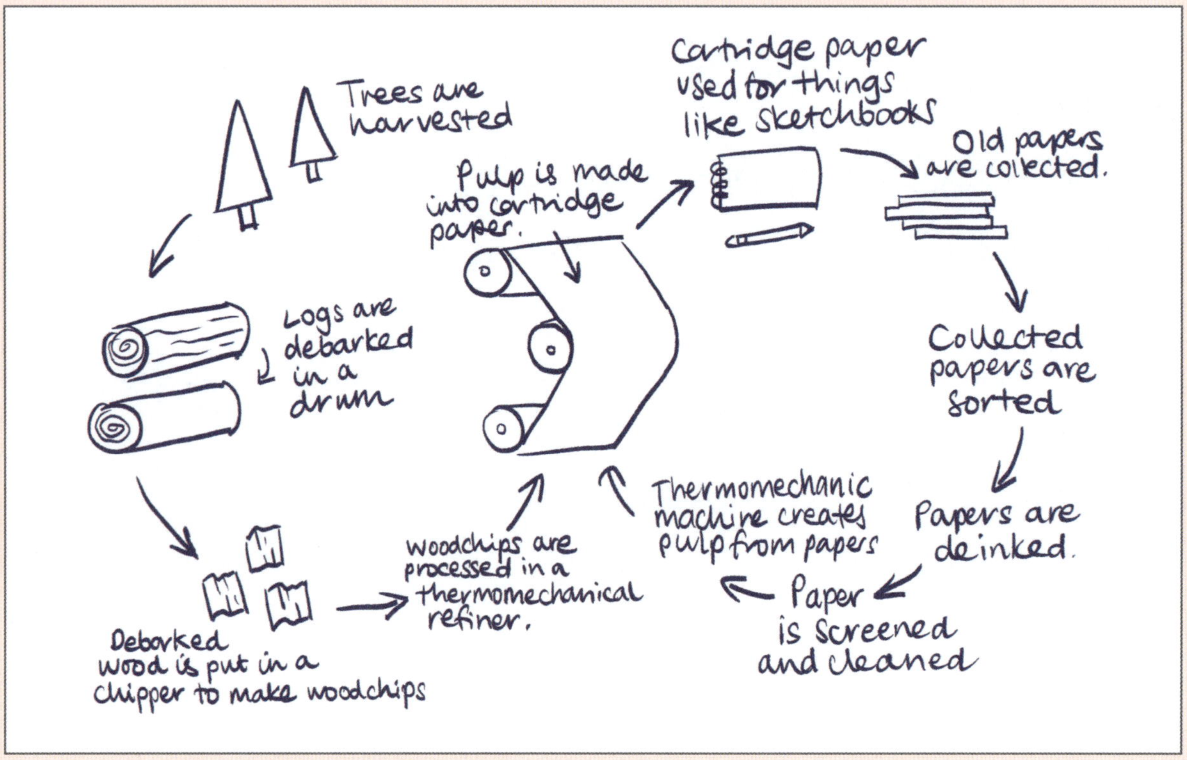

Trees are harvested
Logs are debarked in a drum
Deborked wood is put in a chipper to make woodchips
woodchips are processed in a thermomechanical refiner.
Pulp is made into cartridge paper.
Cartridge paper used for things like sketchbooks
Old papers are collected.
Collected papers are sorted
Papers are deinked.
Paper is screened and cleaned
Thermomechanic machine creates pulp from papers

[6]

TIMBERS

01 **Table 1** shows a range of materials.

Choose **one** of the materials in the table below:

Cartridge paper	Pine	Steel	PVC	Denim

Table 1

My chosen material is: *Pine.*

01.1 Name a specific source of your chosen material.

Trees and forests.

[1]

Exam tip

Make sure that you do what the question says and use notes and sketches in your answer for a possible maximum mark.

01.2 In the box below, use notes and sketches to explain how your chosen material is converted from its primary source into a usable form.

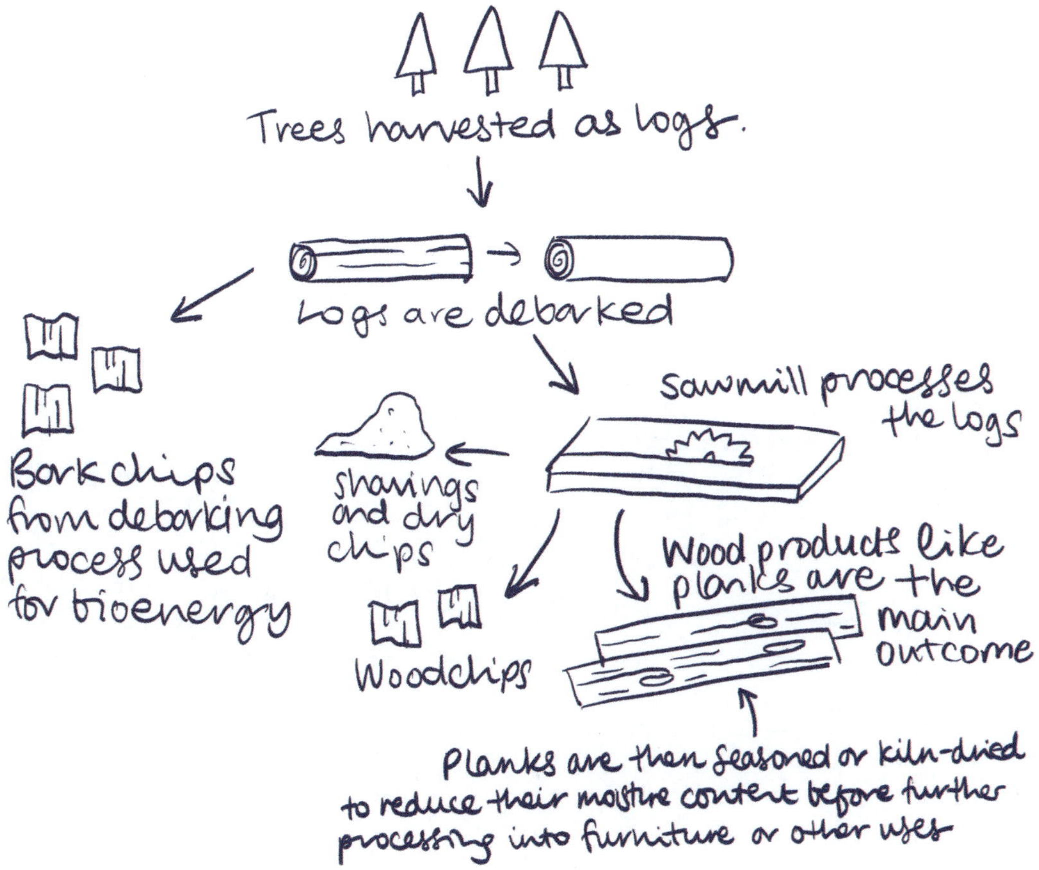
Trees harvested as logs.
Logs are debarked
Bark chips from debarking process used for bioenergy
Sawmill processes the logs
shavings and dry chips
Woodchips
Wood products like planks are the main outcome
Planks are then seasoned or kiln-dried to reduce their moisture content before further processing into furniture or other uses

[6]

3.2.4

SOURCES AND ORIGINS

METALS

01 **Table 1** shows a range of materials.

Choose **one** of the materials in the table below:

Cartridge paper	Pine	Steel	PVC	Denim

Table 1

My chosen material is: *Steel.*

01.1 Name a specific source of your chosen material.

Rocks, (iron) ore and the ground.

[1]

01.2 In the box below, use notes and sketches to explain how your chosen material is converted from its primary source into a usable form.

Exam tip

Make sure that you do what the question says and use notes and sketches in your answer for a possible maximum mark.

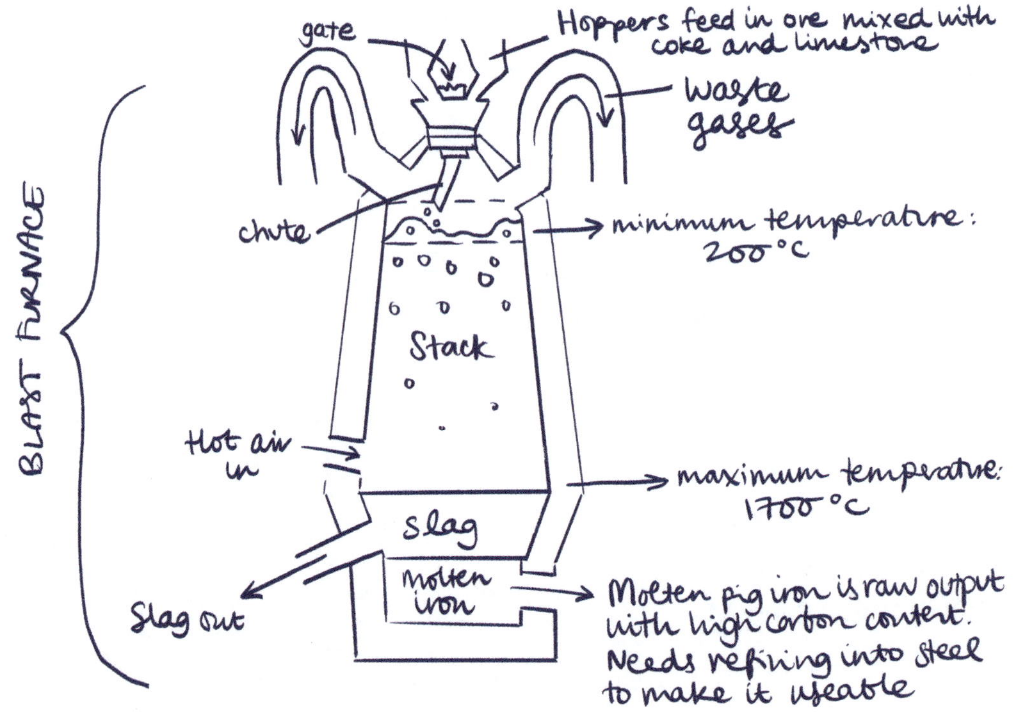

[6]

POLYMERS

01 **Table 1** shows a range of materials.

Choose **one** of the materials in the table below:

Cartridge paper	Pine	Steel	PVC	Denim

Table 1

My chosen material is: *PVC.*

01.1 Name a specific source of your chosen material.

Oil.

[1]

Exam tip

Make sure that you do what the question says and use notes and sketches in your answer for a possible maximum mark.

01.2 In the box below, use notes and sketches to explain how your chosen material is converted from its primary source into a usable form.

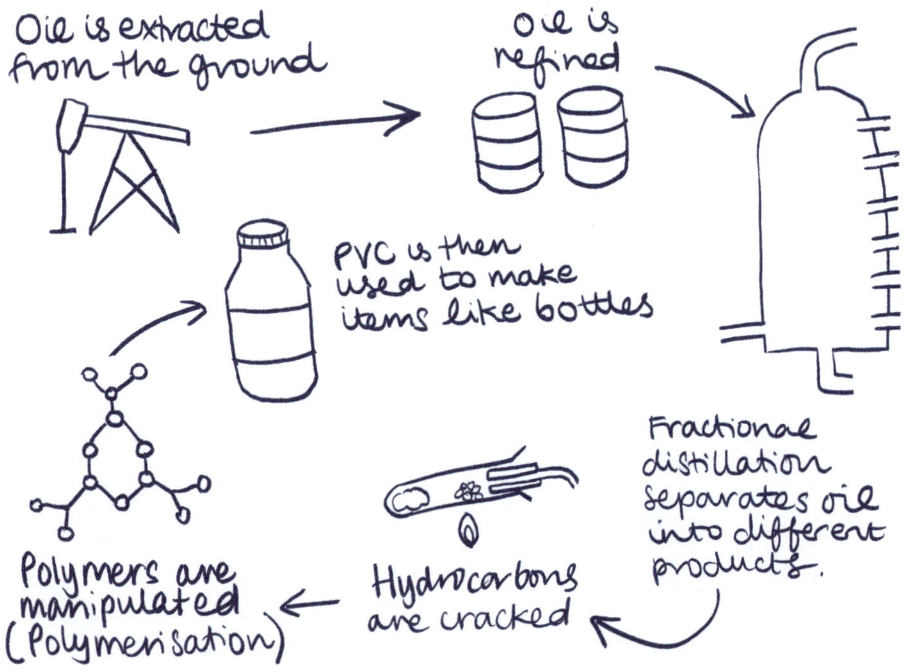

Oil is extracted from the ground
Oil is refined
PVC is then used to make items like bottles
Fractional distillation separates oil into different products.
Hydrocarbons are cracked
Polymers are manipulated (Polymerisation)

[6]

Exam tip

Remember to draw more than just the fractional distillation tower on its own.

3.2.4

SOURCES AND ORIGINS

TEXTILES

01 **Table 1** shows a range of materials.
Choose **one** of the materials in the table below:

Cartridge paper	Pine	Steel	PVC	Denim

Table 1

My chosen material is: *Denim.*

01.1 Name a specific source of your chosen material.

Cotton plants or bols.

[1]

Exam tip

Make sure that you do what the question says and use notes and sketches in your answer for a possible maximum mark.

01.2 In the box below, use notes and sketches to explain how your chosen material is converted from its primary source into a usable form.

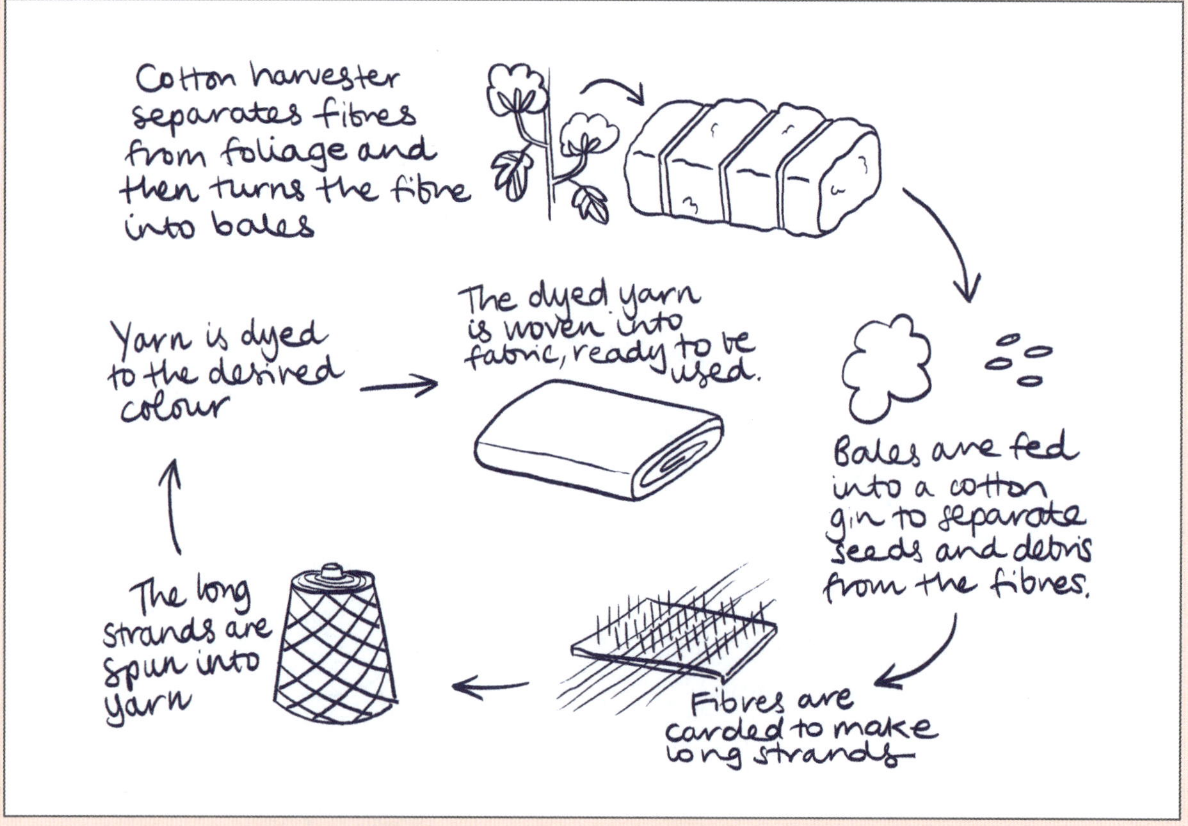

Cotton harvester separates fibres from foliage and then turns the fibre into bales
Bales are fed into a cotton gin to separate seeds and debris from the fibres.
Fibres are carded to make long strands
The long strands are spun into yarn
Yarn is dyed to the desired colour
The dyed yarn is woven into fabric, ready to be used.

[6]

02 Complete **one** row of the table below:

Specific material	Raw source	Conversion process from raw to stock form	Stock form
Acrylic / PMMA			
Beech			
Cardboard			
Polyester			
Aluminium			

[3]

03 Choose **one** material conversion process in the table below:

Wood pulping	Seasoning	Smelting	Fractional distillation	Spinning of thread or yarn

My chosen conversion process is: ....

In the box below, use notes and sketches to explain how your chosen material is converted from its primary source into a usable form.

[6]

Total

/ 9

Answers

See ***page 75*** *for the responses to these questions for each material area.*

3.2.5

USING AND WORKING WITH MATERIALS

PROPERTIES OF MATERIALS

*You should have knowledge and understanding of forces and stresses for at least **one** material category.*

01 **Table 1** shows a range of commercial products made from different materials with different physical properties.

Paper and board artists pad	**Wooden chopping board**	**Metal frying pan**

Polymer soft drinks bottle	**Textile tea towel**	**Electrical wire**

Table 1

01.1 Choose **one** product from the table.

Electrical wire.

01.2 Describe **one** physical property that makes the main construction material suitable for your chosen product.

Electrical wire must be a good conductor of electricity so it can flow along a wire from one point to another in a circuit to another, turning electrical and electronic circuits on or off.

[2]

Insulators

The polymer covering around the copper wire is an **insulator**. It stops electricity from moving from one wire to another when they touch by shielding them.

Do you remember?

Properties of materials is not just about **physical properties**. Materials are also selected for products based on their **working properties** or properties when the product is in use.
See **page 36** for more information.

Exam tip

See **page 56** for alternative responses for each commercial product given above.

02 **Table 2** shows a range of commercial products made from different materials chosen for their different working properties.

		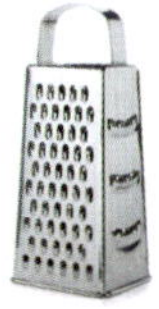
Paper flyer	**Wooden shoe rack**	**Metal cheese grater**
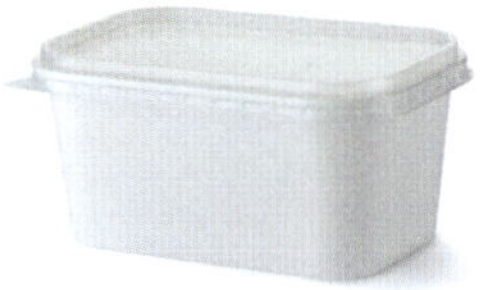		
Polymer margarine container		**Textile socks**

Table 2

02.1 Choose **one** product from the table.

....

02.2 Describe **one** working / mechanical property that makes the identified main material suitable for your chosen product.

....

....

....

....

....

....

[2]

Total

/ 2

Answers

*See **page 57** for the responses to these questions for each material area.*

3.2.5

USING AND WORKING WITH MATERIALS

PROPERTIES OF MATERIALS

Alternative material responses to Question 01 on **page 54**.

Alternative material responses to Question 01 on **page 54**.

01.1 *Paper and board artists pad.*

01.2 *The paper in the drawing pad needs to be absorbent to soak up moisture from paint and pens. Some paper is bleed proof which is specially treated to make it less absorbent, so marker pens do not 'run'.*

01.1 *Wooden chopping board.*

01.2 *The chopping board needs to be a poor thermal conductor if used as a pan rest. This is so a hot pan or dish does not burn the worksurface or table cover below.*

01.1 *Metal frying pan.*

01.2 *The metal frying pan needs to be a good conductor so heat transfer from the hob can be used to heat and cook food placed in the pan.*

01.1 *Polymer soft drinks bottle.*

01.2 *The polymer used in the bottle need to be fusible. This means that when heated, it becomes more liquid so that it can be shaped in one piece into a bottle.*

01.1 *Fabric tea towel.*

01.2 *The tea towel needs to be absorbent to soak up water when drying dishes. It also needs to be a poor thermal conductor as sometimes tea towels are used to handle hot things.*

Answers

Answers to question on ***page 55****.*

02

2 marks	Two simple working / mechanical properties of one product clarified in detail.
1 mark	One mark is awarded for a brief correct point made about working / mechanical properties.
0 marks	No attempt or nothing worthy of credit.

Indicative content:

The paper flyer needs to have shear strength so a finger or pin cannot tear through it[1] if mounting.[1] The paper needs to be strong enough to crease and fold[1] without tearing.[1] Needs to support own weight[1] if pinned up / pushed through a letter box.[1]

Wooden shoe rack needs to be tough and durable,[1] to resist knocks and bangs[1] of shoes being placed on it.[1]

The metal grater needs to resist wear and tear of pressure applied[1] to grate cheese.[1] Needs to be hard[1] enough to keep a sharp edge on grater cutters[1] so cheese can be grated time after time.[1]

The polymer used needs to be tough[1] so that the lid can be removed and replaced multiple times / tub can be dropped without splitting[1] potentially contaminating the contents.[1]

The sock fabric needs to be tough and durable[1] to resist lots of washing[1] when it gets dirty.[1] Also resist wear and tear[1] from rubbing in footwear / toenails.[1]

The metal used in the wire needs to be ductile[1] so that it can be drawn out into long wires[1] with no breaks to ensure conductivity.[1]

Marks can be awarded for various alternative correct responses.

3.2.5

USING AND WORKING WITH MATERIALS

MODIFICATION OF PROPERTIES

*You should have knowledge and understanding of how material properties can be modified for at least **one** material category.*

01 Identify **one** way a material can have its properties modified for a specific use.

Describe the process you have chosen.

Modification: *Anodising.*

> **Do you remember?**
>
> In section B of the exam, you are expected to have a more specialist understanding of at least one material area. In this question it is metals, but you may choose to tackle the question from the paper and board, timbers, polymers, or textile material areas.

Description: *Anodising is a modification process used with aluminium to improve the hardness of the surface and possibly change its colour for aesthetic reasons.*

> **Do you remember?**
>
> Aesthetics are about appearance and beauty.

Aluminium is a soft non-ferrous metal that can corrode and dent when handled a lot and bashed about e.g. carabiners and other rock climbing equipment are anodised.

[3]

> **Exam tip**
>
> Use an example if you feel it helps clarify what you are trying to say.

02 Describe **one** modification process used on **one** material area from **Table 1**.

Papers	Timbers	Metals	Polymers	Textiles

Table 1

Chosen material area: *Polymers.*

Description of modification for chosen material area: *Stabilisers need to be added to polymers to stop UV light leaching colour out of polymer products and making the material brittle over time.*

[2]

03 Choose **one** of the modification processes in **Table 2** below.

Using additives	Seasoning	Annealing	Flame retardancy

Table 2

My chosen process is: ....

Describe how your chosen modification process can improve how a material works for a specific purpose.

....

....

....

....

....

....

[3]

04 Products make use of different material properties to ensure they work properly.
Study **Table 3** below:

Product	Beech toy car	Moulded paper pulp egg box	Stainless steel pan	Denim jacket	Melamine plates and dishes
Material property	Tough	Mouldable	Non-ferrous	Hard wearing	Self-coloured

Choose **one** product and explain how the identified material property used makes the product fit for purpose.

My chosen product is: ....

Explanation: ....

....

....

....

....

[3]

Total
/ 6

☹ 😐 ☺

Answers

*See **page 77** for the responses to these questions for each material area.*

3.2.5

USING AND WORKING WITH MATERIALS

SHAPING AND FORMING

You should have knowledge and understanding of shaping and forming techniques for at least ***one*** *material category.*

01 Give **two** specific ways of cutting materials.

Cutting method 1: *Sawing.*

Cutting method 2: *Using pinking shears.*

[2]

Do you remember?

Other cutting methods and terms you will have used are: filing, slicing, chopping, shearing and drilling.

02 Define the term 'abrasion' and give an example of where it can be evidenced when working with materials.

Definition: *Abrasion is a process of wearing something away.*

Example where abrasion is found when working with materials:

Abrasion is found over time on fabric clothing where small balls (pills) of fabric form on the surface of a textile garment as surfaces rub together.

[2]

Exam tip

This type of question allows for responses about how a product might wear e.g. moving surfaces in a mechanism as well as how abrasion may be used to create a smooth surface, e.g. sanding.

03 Explain how materials can be shaped or formed using addition. Give an example of addition to clarify your answer.

Addition is a process where one material is added to another. Veneer can be added to chipboard to create a worksurface. This can be used in kitchens for food preparation as it is heat proof and sterile / easy to clean.

[3]

Exam tip

Explain questions like this want you to set out reasons in your answer.

Don't be afraid to use extra detail if you can, to make sure you get all available marks. This response is an example from the timbers specialism.

04 Name **one** way a circular hole can be made in a piece of material in a single machining operation.

....

[1]

05 All materials are shaped and formed to create useful products.

Choose **one** of the shape or forming techniques in the table below and complete the appropriate row.

Shape and form technique	Material category used with	Explanation of technique
Perforation		
Planing		
Turning		
Deforming		
Piping		

[3]

Total / 4

Answers

04 *Drilling, piercing, punching, laser cutting, routing.*[1]

05 ***One mark** for an appropriate material category identified.*

***Two marks** for an explanation of the selected technique. One mark for up to two simple correct points. Two marks for a clarified correct point.*

Mark one row only.

Shape and form technique	Material category used with	Explanation of technique
Perforation	*Paper, card, textiles*	*Small holes in a line are formed to create a weakness in the material so it easily tears e.g. tissue box lid.*
Planing	*Timbers*	*A plane removes shavings of wood to create a smooth finish on an edge or face of a piece of wood.*
Turning	*Timbers, metals, polymers*	*Material can be turned on a metal lathe or a woodwork lathe to create concentric shapes and forms e.g., spindles, shafts and bowls.*
Deforming	*Papers and boards, textiles and polymers*	*Papers and boards can be embossed or debossed to create a relief feature. Non-woven textiles, like felt, can be steamed and drape formed e.g., hats. Polymers can be drape formed, but we normally call it vacuum forming or blow moulding.*
Piping	*Textiles*	*This forming technique involves folding fabric into a seam to make the edge stand out and become tougher / more resistant to wear e.g., cushions and seat upholstery.*

3.2.6 STOCK FORMS, TYPES AND SIZES

*You should have knowledge and understanding of different stock forms, types and sizes available for at least **one** material category.*

01 Define the term stock form.
Give an example in your answer.

When you buy a material in a commercially available or standard form / size that is not specially made for you, for example, 6mm MDF sheet.

[3]

Exam tip

Don't forget to do what the question asks e.g. give an example.

02 Give **two** benefits of purchasing materials in stock forms.

Benefit 1: *You can purchase the most common sizes that fit with most other products and tools.*

Benefit 2: *When you buy a material in a stock form, it will have been manufactured in vast quantities all at once meaning that it should be available at a lower cost than ordering a special size or form, requiring machines to be specially set up to make a custom order.*

[2]

03 The shoe rack in **Figure 1** is to be manufactured using metal tube available in standard stock lengths of 4 metres.

The shoe rack uses twelve lengths of metal tube for the horizontal rails to support the shoes.

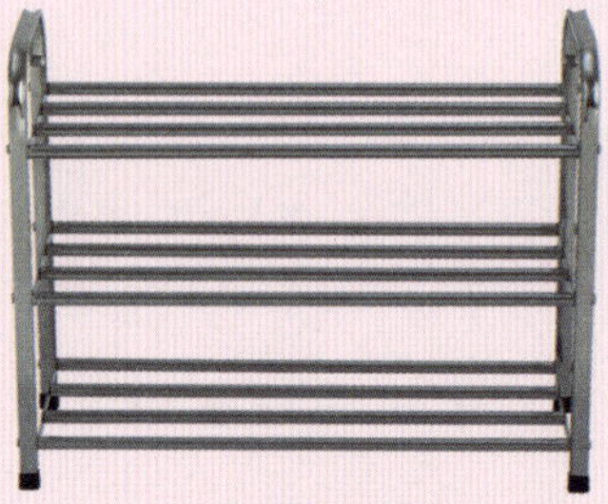

Figure 1

Each length is 700 mm long.

How many standard form lengths of 4 metres will be required to make **one** shoe rack?

Show your working.

4 metres ÷ 0.7 = 5 lengths of 700 mm tube with 0.5 metres wastage.

To make 1 shoe rack: 5 rails from each length of stock form material and 2 lengths from a 3rd length.

MY ANSWER IS: 3 lengths will be needed.

[3]

Exam tip

Make your final answer really clear for the examiner to find.

04 Describe how stock forms of materials make reordering materials easier.

....

....

....

....

....

....

[3]

Figure 2

05 The mirror frame in **Figure 2** is to be manufactured from six pieces of wood moulding. Calculate the angle that each piece will need to be cut at to fit together seamlessly. Show your working.

....

....

....

....

[2]

Total

/ 5

Answers

04

3 marks	At least two points clarified in detail about how stock forms make reordering easier.
2 marks	One point clarified in detail about how stock forms make reordering easier.
1 mark	One simple correct point made.
0 marks	No attempt or nothing worthy of credit.

Indicative content

When someone requires more standard form materials, they can compare the prices of materials available from different suppliers[1] and get the best deal available / get the materials at the lowest price.[1] Standard sizes are more likely to be in plentiful supply / more readily available.[1]

05 *360° in a circle / 6 pieces = 60°[1] Award both marks for correct answer.*

3.2.7 SCALES OF PRODUCTION

01 The products in **Table 1** below are all produced in different scales.
Give the name of the scale of production most appropriate for the product or component in the picture
Fill in the space below each picture with your answer.

Product or component			
Scale of production	*Continuous*	*One-off / bespoke*	*Batch*

[3]

02 Give **one** advantage and **one** disadvantage of mass production.

Advantage: *Good for producing identical items in large quantities.*

Disadvantage: *Expensive to buy equipment for mass production.*

Exam tip

Avoid one-word answers like fast or cheap.

[2]

03 Describe the ways in which prototype production differs from continuous production.
Give specific examples of products in your answer.

Prototype or one-off production is used to make a product for a specific customer e.g. a wedding cake or wedding dress. The process involves a lot of personal attention and high-level craftsmanship to ensure the product is just what the client wants.

Continuous production is used for relatively simple everyday products and components in daily use. There is a continuous demand, and the product specifications don't often change or evolve over time e.g., aerosols for paints, deodorants and sprays.

Exam tip

A very detailed response considering both methods of production. Very clear specific examples are given.

[6]

Exam tip

Remember that higher mark questions are marked differently compared to shorter questions. The mark scheme will use banded marking descriptors for longer answer questions where the examiner will have to make a judgement to award a mark within a range.

04 Give **one** advantage and **one** disadvantage of batch production.

Advantage: ....

....

Disadvantage: ....

....

[2]

05 **Figure 1** below shows a modern TV.

Figure 1

05.1 Name the most suitable scale of production for the TV.

....

[1]

05.2 Give reasons why the scale of production given in **05.1** is most suitable for the TV.

....

....

....

....

[3]

Total / 6

☹ 😐 ☺

Answers

04 One mark for each correct answer.

***Advantages:** Equipment is flexible and can be easily changed for other products.*[1]
Cheaper to produce a batch than a single product at a time.[1]

***Disadvantages:** Downtime where equipment must be reset for another product.* [1]
Difficult to personalise a particular product.[1]

05.1 Mass production.[1]

05.2

3 marks	At least two points clarified in detail about the scale of production given in part 05.1.
2 marks	One point clarified in detail about the scale of production given in part 05.1.
1 mark	One simple correct point about the scale of production.
0 marks	No attempt or nothing worthy of credit.

Indicative content:

- *Product is demanded by customers in larger numbers, possibly due to global marketing.*
- *A higher production level is required to sell the products at a competitive price.*
- *Many identical products are required.*
- *A mass production run may continue for months or years until the TV is replaced by a newer model with better technology.*

3.2.8

SPECIALIST TECHNIQUES AND PROCESSES

PRODUCTION AIDS

01 What is a template?

A template is a shaped piece of material e.g. card that you can draw or cut around to repeat a shape outline several times.

[2]

Do you remember?

- You draw or cut around a **template**.
- You draw or cut inside a **stencil**.
- **Patterns** are a type of template to draw or cut around, or as a three-dimensional positive shape used to create a mould for casting.

02.1 Define the term **datum point**.

A datum point is a point where all measurements are taken from. It is sometimes called the origin point or reference point.

[2]

02.2 Describe **one** specific example where a datum point needs to be used.

When setting up a laser cutter for use, the laser must be focused and zeroed on a specific point. The software used with the laser cutter then will start manufacturing from that specific point, completing all cutting and/or engraving as per the design file being used. The datum point reduces error and makes the process more accurate so that the base material being cut can be used efficiently to make more parts / products later. This minimises waste.

[2]

03 What is a jig when used in manufacturing operations?
Give **one** example of use.

A jig is a tool that helps save time with marking out. Where more than one part is needed, i.e. it needs to be repeated, it would be time consuming to mark out each part. It may also lead to error and inaccuracies. A jig will guide you to cut, saw or shear in a specific place, or to drill a hole is a specific place.

[3]

Exam tip

Here is a detailed example answering the question fully.

04 Give **one** advantage and **one** disadvantage of using a template.

Advantage: ....

....

....

Disadvantage: ....

....

....

[2 x 2]

05 Explain why datum points need to be used in CAD and CAM.

....

....

....

....

....

....

....

....

[3]

Total /7

☹ 😐 ☺

Answers

04 One mark for each correct answer.

***Advantages:** Templates increase efficiency. They save marking out time. Quicker than drawing out every time. Help with batch production.*

***Disadvantages:** They can get damaged around the edge and lose their accuracy over time. Templates can be easily damaged if they are being cut around so care needs to be taken to use an appropriate material.*

05

3 marks	At least **two points** clarified in detail.
2 marks	One point clarified in detail.
1 mark	One simple correct point.
0 marks	No attempt or nothing worthy of credit.

Indicative content:

- *Needed to increase accuracy in manufacture.*
- *Reduce error having to set up each measurement or cut.*
- *All measurements are taken from the datum point.*
- *Ensure consistency is maintained.*
- *Reduce waste in materials as many parts can be nested next to each other e.g. using a laser cutter.*

3.2.8

SPECIALIST TECHNIQUES AND PROCESSES

TOOLS AND EQUIPMENT

*You should have knowledge and understanding of the tools, equipment and processes associated with at least **one** material category.*

01 Wastage is commonly avoided by manufacturers.

01.1 Explain what the term 'wastage' means when working with materials.

Wastage is off-cuts or a surplus of materials that cannot be used for another purpose. Waste can also be defined as any process or raw material that does not add any value to a product.

[2]

01.2 **Table 1** shows different methods of wastage.

Die cutting	Sawing	Shearing	Drilling	Milling

Table 1

Explain how **one** of the wastage methods is used to form a product.

Die cutting uses a series of blades that are forced under pressure into a material such as paper, card, rubber or fabric. You need a die cutting machine to ensure pressure is applied evenly to the blades and to ensure the cut is consistent.

Exam tip

Questions like **01.2** can be answered for several materials. There is not always just one material that can be used to answer a question.

Other possible responses include:

Sawing involves making a cut using a blade with teeth. Sawing is used to cut one piece of a material from a larger piece. Sometimes sawing is used to cut a shape out of a sheet material like MDF or acrylic.

Shearing is a process that does not involve a single blade, but two cutting surfaces that move past each other to create a scissor action e.g. scissors.

Drilling involves creating a hole in a material. Usually this involves a drill. A drill bit is placed in a chuck which spins as it is lowered into the surface of a material. Drills can cut blind or through holes.

Milling is a process a bit like drilling in that it uses a rotating cutter being slowly pushed into a material such as aluminium or steel in either an X, Y or Z axis. Unlike a drill, the side of the cutter rather than just the tip is used. Usually, the speeds involved are higher to create a smooth finish.

[2]

02 **Table 2** has pictures of tools used to cut and shape materials.

Cordless drill	**Pinking shears**	**Craft knife**

Table 2

Explain how **one** of the tools **Table 2** is used to shape material.

My chosen tool: ....

Explanation: ....

....

....

[2]

03 State what the term 'addition' means when working with materials.

Give **one** example in your answer.

....

....

....

[2]

Total

/ 4

Answers

02 Use the following levels-based mark scheme for Question 02.

2 marks	One point clarified in detail or two simple points of explanation.
1 mark	One simple point of explanation.
0 marks	No attempt or nothing worthy of credit.

Indicative content:

- ***Cordless drill:*** *Used to drill either a through hole or blind hole in materials such as wood, metal, and plastic. Drill has variable speeds for different sized drill bits and forward and reverse functions if the drill gets stuck.*
- ***Pinking shears:*** *Used on fabric to stop material edges from fraying. Particularly useful on loose weave type fabrics.*
- ***Craft knife:*** *Used for cutting fibres in materials such as paper and card. Creates a precise cut which is not possible with scissors.*

03

1 mark	Correct meaning of the term addition.

1 mark	One correct example.

Indicative content:

Meaning	Where one material is added to another.
Examples	Brazing, welding, lamination, soldering, 3D printing, batik, sewing, bonding, and printing.

3.2.8

SPECIALIST TECHNIQUES AND PROCESSES

TOLERANCES, COMMERCIAL PROCESSES AND QUALITY CONTROL

*You should have knowledge and understanding of tolerances, commercial processes and quality control associated with at least **one** material category.*

Do you remember?

The reason for a tolerance is to ensure consistency in making, but also that it is really difficult to make every part 100% identical all the time.

01 Explain how materials are cut and shaped to a tolerance.

When materials are cut to a tolerance, an allowance is made for the cut being slightly inaccurate. You accept the cut being slightly out of position. This could be 0.5 mm either side of a line. If you were drilling a hole, say 6mm, you might allow a tolerance of +/-0.5mm. This means the hole can be between 6.5mm and 5.5mm in diameter.

[2]

02 Define the term 'quality control'.
Give **one** example in your answer.

Quality control is the process of making checks when a product or part is being manufactured.
An example is checking the alignment of a repeating pattern on a roll of fabric.

[3]

03 The table below shows techniques used to ensure quality control when making products.

Go / no go jig	**Depth stop**	**UV exposure time**

Choose **one** technique and using notes and sketches explain how it is used in the manufacture of products.

My chosen technique is: *UV exposure time.*

UV exposure time is a quality control technique used when making Printed Circuit Boards (PCBs).
It refers to how long a PCB with a photosensitive coating is left in a UV light box to develop the circuit board tracks. Exposure time is usually 3–7 minutes.
Other examples of quality control include registration marks in printing, and etching times in PCB manufacture.

[5]

PCB is placed into UV lightbox
Lightbulbs

Exam tip

Make sure you use notes and sketches in this type of question to give yourself the best chance of maximum marks.

04 Choose **one** of the commercial processes in the table below.

Offset lithography	**Turning**	**Injection moulding**	**Weaving**	**Flow soldering**

My chosen process is: ....

Using notes and sketches, describe the process you have named above.

[6]

Do you remember?

Other commercial processes include pick and place assembly, flow soldering, blow moulding and extrusion. You also need to be prepared for a question on school based processes including vacuum forming, creasing, pressing, drape forming, bending, folding and casting.

Total / 6

Answers

04 *See **page 72** for the responses to this question for each commercial process.*

5–6 marks	Very detailed notes **and** sketches clearly showing sound understanding of chosen process.
3–4 marks	Good notes **and / or** sketches of the chosen process.
1–2 marks	Limited note(s) **or** sketch matching the chosen process.
0 marks	No attempt or nothing worthy of credit.

ANSWERS

Offset lithography

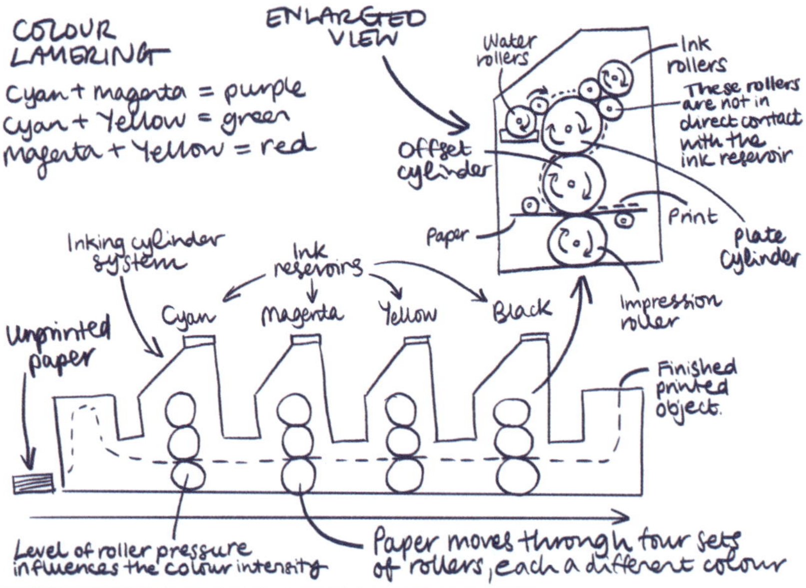
COLOUR LAYERING
Cyan + magenta = purple
Cyan + Yellow = green
Magenta + Yellow = red
ENLARGED VIEW
Water rollers
Ink rollers
These rollers are not in direct contact with the ink reservoir
Offset cylinder
Print
Plate cylinder
Paper
Impression roller
Inking cylinder system
Ink reservoirs
Cyan
Magenta
Yellow
Black
Unprinted paper
Finished printed object.
Level of roller pressure influences the colour intensity
Paper moves through four sets of rollers, each a different colour

Turning

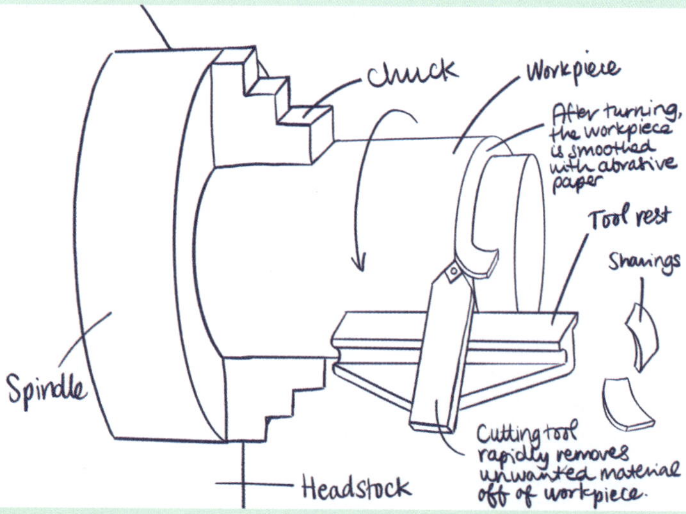
Chuck
Workpiece
After turning, the workpiece is smoothed with abrasive paper
Tool rest
Shavings
Spindle
Headstock
Cutting tool rapidly removes unwanted material off of workpiece.

Injection moulding

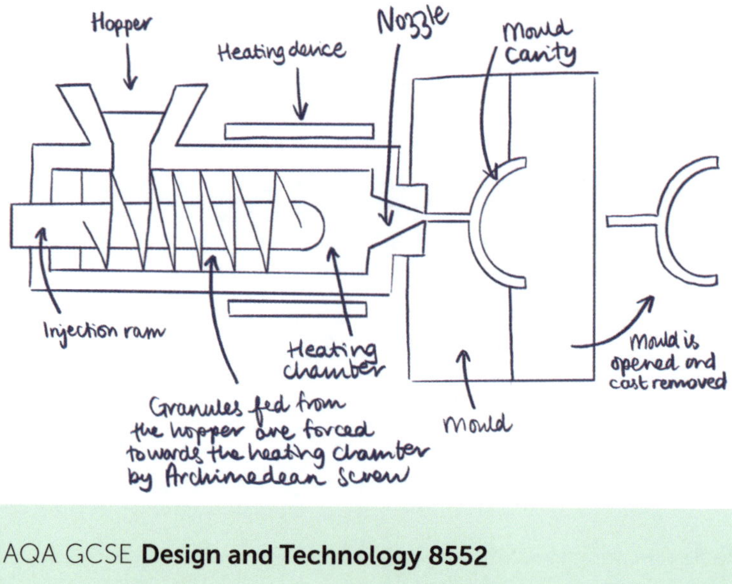
Hopper
Heating device
Nozzle
Mould cavity
Injection ram
Heating chamber
Granules fed from the hopper are forced towards the heating chamber by Archimedean screw
Mould
Mould is opened and cast removed

Weaving

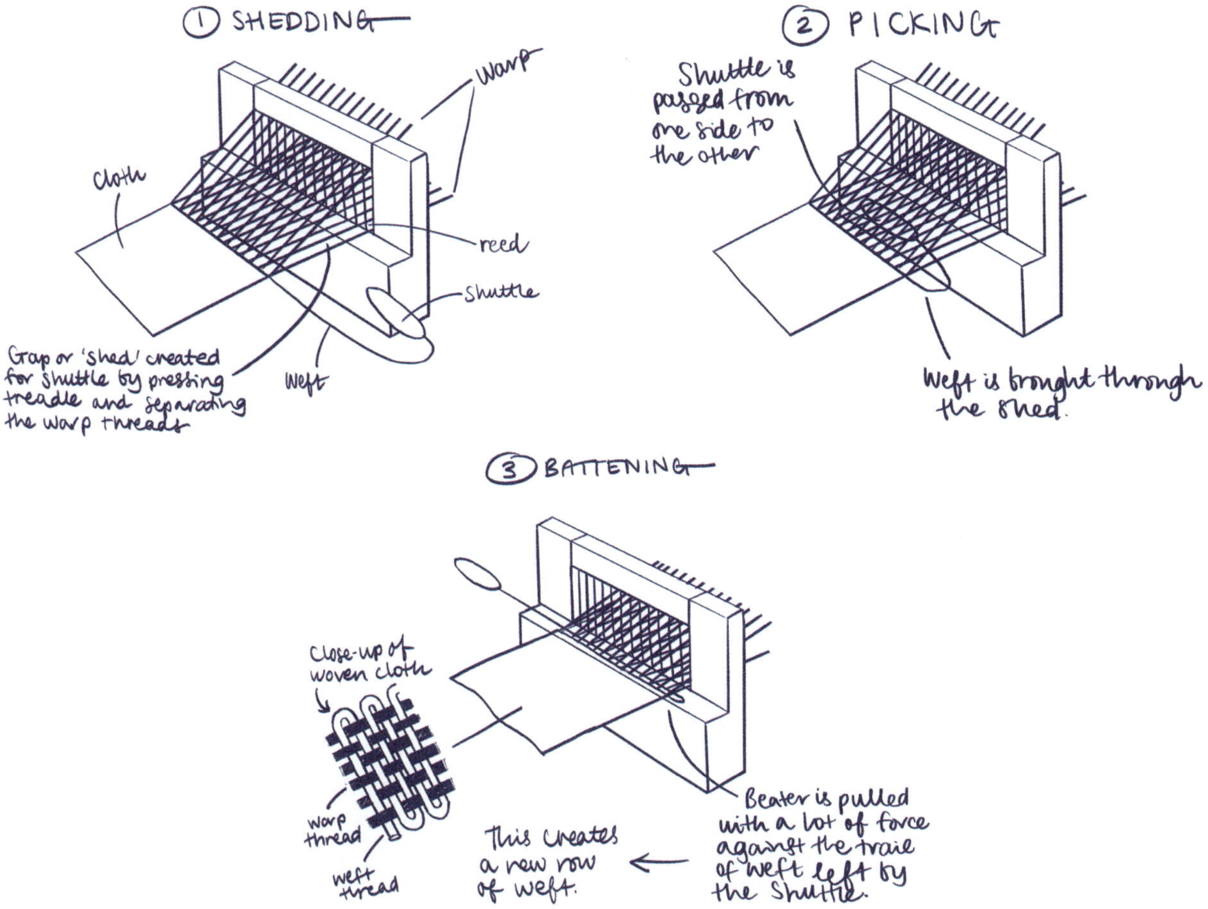

① SHEDDING
warp
cloth
reed
shuttle
Gap or 'shed' created for shuttle by pressing treadle and separating the warp threads
weft
② PICKING
Shuttle is passed from one side to the other
Weft is brought through the shed.
③ BATTENING
Close-up of woven cloth
warp thread
weft thread
This creates a new row of weft.
Beater is pulled with a lot of force against the trail of weft left by the shuttle.

Flow soldering

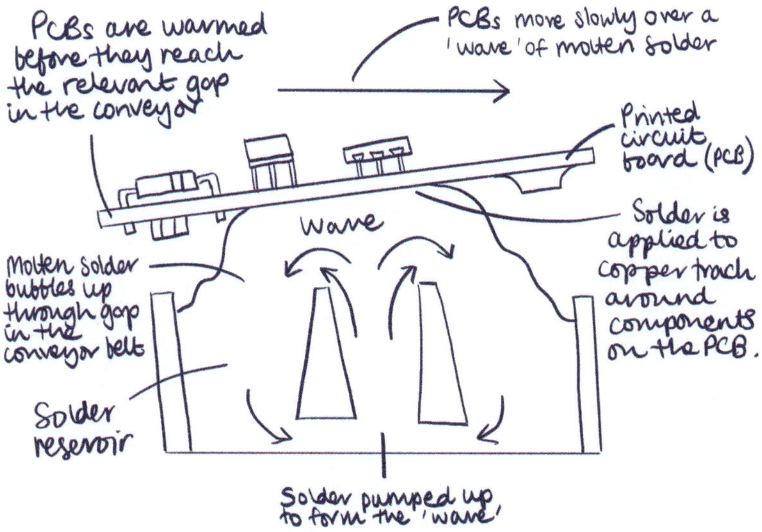

PCBs are warmed before they reach the relevant gap in the conveyor
PCBs move slowly over a 'wave' of molten solder
Printed circuit board (PCB)
wave
Solder is applied to copper track around components on the PCB.
Molten solder bubbles up through gap in the conveyor belt
Solder reservoir
Solder pumped up to form the 'wave'

3.2.9 SURFACE TREATMENTS AND FINISHES

*You should have knowledge and understanding of surface treatments and finishes for at least **one** material category.*

Exam tip

Thoughtful answers will make sure good quality examples are included if required.

01 Explain, with examples, why finishes are applied to materials for aesthetic reasons.

Finishes are applied to change the colour of material e.g., painting a child's wooden toy. Sometimes a finish can be applied to enhance the natural appearance of a material e.g. varnishing or staining to bring out the grain of wood. On a piece of fabric, a finish e.g. batik can be applied to create a decorative dye pattern.

[3]

02 Describe **two** measures you would take to prepare a material before applying a finish.

Method 1: *The surface of most materials needs to be dust, dirt and grease free or you will get lumps in the surface and it will not be smooth.*

Method 2: *Some materials, for example woods and metals, need a primer and undercoat to make sure the topcoat (the actual paint finish you see) sticks properly and does not flake off over time.*

[2 x 2]

Do you remember?

Sometimes finishes need to be greasy. In mechanisms, grease and oil can be used as a surface finish for functional reasons to allow moving parts to slide over each other to reduce wear and avoid overheating.

03 Finishes can be applied in a variety of ways. Three ways of applying finishes have been given in **Table 1**. Choose **one** of the ways of applying a finish and answer the questions below:

Brushing	Spraying	Dipping

Table 1

My chosen way of applying a finish is: *Brushing.*

03.1 An advantage of my chosen application method is: *Paint brushes are relatively cheap compared to expensive spraying systems. They do not need power as they are not limited by the length of a cable and can be used almost anywhere.*

[2]

Exam tip

'Cheap' must be explained as shown for a mark.

03.2 A disadvantage of my chosen application method is: *Brushes can lose hairs which can then get stuck in the finish applied e.g. hairs in a paint finish and can create unsightly flaws. Brushes also need cleaning so that they can be reused.*

[2]

04 Describe **two** ways that finishes are applied to materials for aesthetic reasons.

Reason 1:

....

....

....

Reason 2:

....

....

....

[2 x 2]

05 Explain, with examples, why finishes are applied to materials for functional reasons.

....

....

....

....

....

....

....

[4]

Total

/ 8

Answers

04

2 marks	One point clarified in detail or two simple points of explanation.
1 mark	One simple point of explanation.
0 marks	No attempt or nothing worthy of credit.

Indicative content:

- ***Colour:*** *Change the colour of a material to suit preferences. Includes printing and vinyl decals.*
- ***Texture:*** *Change the surface from rough to smooth or smooth to rough. Includes embossing and debossing.*
- ***Sheen:*** *Gloss, satin or matt for a shiny or dull finish. Includes varnishing and UV varnish.*

05

3–4 marks	Two or more functional points considered in detail. **Must include examples for maximum marks**.
1–2 marks	One simple or two brief functional points correctly considered. May or may not use examples to support answer.
0 marks	No attempt or nothing worthy of credit.

Indicative content:

- *Tanalising to inhibit fungal and insect attack on timbers e.g., woodworm.*
- *Oils and grease to lubricate rubbing surfaces and moving parts e.g., a gearbox.*
- *UV varnishing e.g., on paper and card to add durability and protection.*
- *Flame retardant finishes on textiles e.g., upholstery finishes in the home.*
- *To stop corrosion (rusting) on metals e.g., dip/powder coating steel, anodising aluminium.*

ANSWERS

02 There is one mark for each correct column response. All responses must be in the same row. If more than one row attempted, mark best row.

Specific material	Source	Conversion process from raw to stock form	Stock form
Acrylic / PMMA	*Crude oil*	*Fractional distillation/polymerisation*	*Rod, tube, granules powder, sheet*
Beech	*Tree / forest*	*Felling, seasoning*	*Plank, veneer*
Cardboard	*Tree / wood pulp*	*Debarking, pulping, sizing*	*Sheet, roll, ply*
Polyester	*Crude oil / petroleum*	*Fractional distillation, spinning, twisting*	*Thread, yarn*
Aluminium	*Bauxite / rocks / ore*	*Alloying/smelting*	*Ingot, rod, tube, angle, sheet, plate*

03 This type of question will use best fit description bands:

5–6 marks	A thorough understanding using notes and sketches showing understanding of how a chosen process converts a raw material into a workable form.
3–4 marks	A good understanding using notes and/or sketches showing understanding of how a chosen process converts a raw material into a workable form.
1–2 marks	A basic understanding with one or two points made in note or sketch form.
0 marks	No attempt or nothing worthy of credit.

Indicative content:

Wood pulping	Seasoning	Smelting	Fractional distillation	Spinning of thread or yarn
Key points	Key points	Key points	Key points	Key points
• *Wood debarked.* • *Added to chemicals.* • *Cooked in vats.* • *Bleaching of pulp to get colour.*	• *Air seasoning.* • *Kiln seasoning.* • *Drying to reduce moisture content.* • *20% moisture content for exterior use.* • *10% moisture content for interior use.*	• *Bayer process.* • *Bauxite is crushed and melted.* • *Aluminium extracted by smelting, not heating ore alone.*	• *Crude oil is heated.* • *Different components separated out at different temperatures as each have different boiling points.*	• *Separation of fibres and laying them out in line.* • *Carding and combing to produce straight fibres.* • *Fibres fed through rollers where they are twisted.*

ANSWERS

03

3 marks	At least two points clarified in detail about how the chosen process can improve how a material works.
2 marks	One point clarified in detail about how the chosen process can improve how a material works.
1 mark	One simple point of improvement named.
0 marks	No attempt or nothing worthy of credit.

Indicative content — Using additives

- A photosensitive additive/layer is added to the copper layer on a PCB.
- The PCB is then exposed to UV light causing a chemical change in selected areas (tracks) of the PCB board.
- The PCB board is then developed in a sodium hydroxide or ferric chloride solution so that the unwanted copper between the circuit tracks is removed, creating a precise electrical circuit.

Other examples of modification that could be considered include:

- Additives to paper and board to prevent moisture damage (sizing).
- Seasoning of timber to reduce moisture content.
- Annealing of metals to reduce hardness and increase ductility.
- Stabilisers and plasticisers in polymers to prevent degradation, e.g. UV stabilisers or improve flexibility.

04

3 marks	At least two points clarified in detail about how the chosen material property makes the product fit for purpose.
2 marks	One point clarified in detail about how the chosen process can improve how a material works. One point clarified in detail about how the chosen material property used makes the product fit for purpose.
1 mark	One simple reference to a chosen material property.
0 marks	No attempt or nothing worthy of credit.

Indicative content

- Toy car (tough beech) – so it can resist being dropped and roughly treated by a child during play. Splinters should not be produced which present safety issues.
- Egg box (moulded paper pulp) – so the exact shape of an egg box can be created by sucking the pulp onto a mould and then dried to create a one-piece holder that supports the fragile egg shape. The moulded design stops the eggs from banging into each other.
- Stainless steel pan (ferrous alloy) - stainless steel does not rust or stain easily and keeps looking good for a long time. Ferrous metals would rust when cooking or placed in a sink or dishwasher but this is prevented by alloying with chromium.
- Denim jacket (hard wearing cotton) – denim is a durable material, resistant to abrasion and won't pill if rubbed. Traditionally used to make long lasting work clothes and overalls.
- Melamine plates and dishes (self-coloured polymer) – the pigment is added during manufacture and can be changed to suit different colour schemes. The colour is the full depth of the product so can't be scratched off and keeps the product looking good when in regular use.

SECTION C

3.3 DESIGNING AND MAKING PRINCIPLES

Information

At least 15% of the exam will assess maths and at least 10% will assess science.

There are 100 marks in total. 20 marks for Section A, 30 for Section B and 50 for Section C.

All questions are mandatory.

All dimensions are in millimetres.

!

You **will** need:
A black pen (and some spares)

You may also use:
An HB pencil, ruler and other normal writing and drawing instruments
A calculator
A protractor

3.3.1 PRIMARY AND SECONDARY DATA

01 Give the name of the research data show in the diagram below.

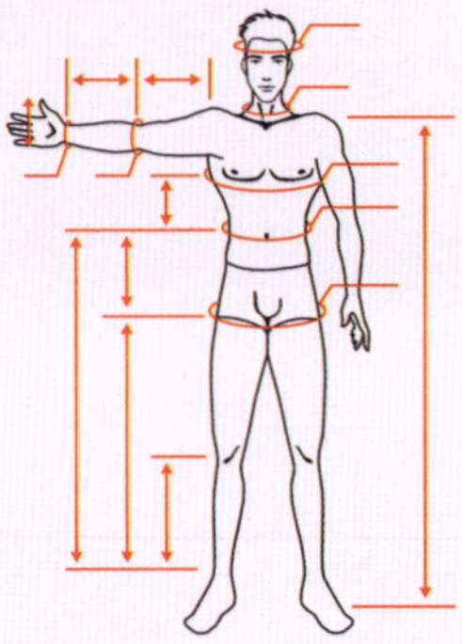

Research data shown is: *Anthropometric data.*

[1]

Exam tip

This is a simple right or wrong answer. Look at the key word.

Do you remember?

You also need to know about ergonomics (the process of designing products and workplaces around people) and how percentiles are used with this sort of data. Most products are designed to fit anyone that falls between the 5th and 95th percentiles in terms of measurements.

02 Define the term 'secondary data' used in research.
Give an example in your answer.

Secondary data is information that has been created by other people that you can use without having to collect and gather it yourself. An example of secondary data is product reviews in magazines and online.

[3]

Exam tip

Don't forget your example!

03 Discuss how focus groups are used in the development of prototypes.

A focus groups is a group of people brought together to answer questions as part of market research to help identify needs and wants in the design of a prototype or product. A focus group is made up of people identified with similar interests or experience to help with market research in a specific problem area. Focus groups are asked questions, but they also have the opportunity to talk about a design problem with each other or possibly test mock ups and prototype solutions.

[4]

Do you remember?

This type of question is likely to use three mark bands: 3–4 marks, 1–2 marks, 0 marks.

04 Define the term 'primary data' used in research.
Give an example in your answer.

....

....

....

....

....

[3]

05 Explain how interviews can be used to inform your design ideas.

....

....

....

....

....

[3]

Total / 6

☹ 😐 ☺

Answers

04 One mark for a relevant example and ...

2 marks	One point clarified in detail or two simple points of explanation.
1 mark	One simple point of explanation.
0 marks	No attempt or nothing worthy of credit.

Indicative content:

- *Primary data is research that you personally collect[1] and is not gathered from a third party[1] or published source.[1]*
- *Examples include, interviews, observations and taking your own measurements.*

05

3 marks	Two points of explanation with one clarified in detail.
2 marks	One point clarified in detail or two simple points of explanation.
1 mark	One simple point of explanation.
0 marks	No attempt or nothing worthy of credit.

Indicative content:

- *You can find out the needs and wants of potential customers by speaking to them and asking general or focused questions.[1]*
- *You can find out the opinions of people who want or need the product.[1]*
- *Interviews and questioning can identify a gap in the market[1]*
- *It can help to gather culturally sensitive feedback when trading internationally.[1]*
- *Interviews allow potential clients to provide lots of information that could be recorded of filmed for later analysis.[1]*

3.3.1 INVESTIGATION AND DESIGN BRIEF

01 Define a design **need**.

A design need is something that is essential to a project and not negotiable. It must be addressed during the design process. For example, reflective clothing for a cyclist or an adjustable table for a wheelchair user can be considered as design needs.

[1]

> **Exam tip**
>
> Give examples to help show understanding even though they are not required by the question.

02 Describe **two** research techniques that can be used to identify problems and needs before starting design ideas.

Research method 1: *The internet could be used to find commercial products that may already exist to solve the problem. Sometimes existing products that solve one problem can be adapted to satisfy the needs and requirements of a different problem.*

Research method 2: *Client interviews or surveys could be carried out to find out specific client needs and wants to help inform other research or investigations before design ideas start.*

[2 × 2]

> **Exam tip**
>
> Avoid one word or very short answers where two or more marks are available.

03 Explain how a manufacturing specification is used in the manufacture of prototype products.

A manufacturing specification records vital information about materials and components to be used to make a prototype or product. It can show the sizes and quantities of materials and components used. This detail is sometimes called a parts list or a cutting list. Other detail may show stages and the sequence of production stages involved in how the product may be made.

[3]

> **Do you remember?**
>
> Other documents that are good evidence for a manufacturing specification are:
> - Working drawings
> - Patterns and plans
> - Schematics

04 Explain how market research can help in an investigation of design ideas.

....

....

....

....

....

[3]

05 Explain how a design specification is used to create effective design ideas.

....

....

....

....

....

[3]

Total

/ 6

☹ 😐 ☺

Answers

04

3 marks	Two points of explanation with one clarified in detail.
2 marks	One point clarified in detail or two simple points of explanation.
1 mark	One simple point of explanation.
0 marks	No attempt or nothing worthy of credit.

Indicative content:

- *Find out what is already available on the market*[1] *and identify strengths and weaknesses.*[1]
- *Get an idea of price for existing products*[1] *and specifications of existing products that exist.*[1]
- *Who will the customer/client be?*[1]

05

3 marks	Two points of explanation with one clarified in detail.
2 marks	One point clarified in detail or two simple points of explanation.
1 mark	One simple point of explanation.
0 marks	No attempt or nothing worthy of credit.

Indicative content:

- *A design specification takes all the key features of the research and investigation*[1] *and uses them to come up with measurable*[1] *criteria*[1] *to help with designing.*
- *It helps evaluate the product or prototype manufactured.*[1]
- *It helps ensure the prototype or product meets client requirements.*[1]

3.3.2

ENVIRONMENTAL, SOCIAL AND ECONOMIC CHALLENGE

01 Explain how supporting fair trade is good for sustainable business relationships.

> **Do you remember?**
>
> This question also links with Section A, dealing with enterprise.

Fair trade makes sure that farmers and producers get paid a fair price for their goods and services e.g., food products such as coffee and cocoa. A fair price leads to a sustainable business arrangement, where farmers can support their families and workers, not only with food on the table, but better healthcare and education.

[4]

02 Discuss how purchasing the bookcase in the image below may contribute to deforestation, and what can be done to limit the damage that deforestation can do to the environment.

The bookcase is made from wood. This means the raw material source is trees and forests. If trees are cut down irresponsibly, it will lead to deforestation. Manufacturers can make sure that they only use timber sourced from approved sources e.g. FSC where at least one tree is planted for every tree cut down. The bookcase will need packaging, especially if it is sold in flat pack form. If corrugated cardboard is used, this also comes from trees and timber. Cardboard can be made from recycled wood pulp and that will slow the rate at which tress are cut down.

[6]

> **Do you remember?**
>
> Discuss questions ask you to identify key points and look at the question from different angles.
>
> Here, you need to look at the contribution to deforestation and what can be done to slow or stop deforestation.

03 Discuss how electronic products in the home contribute to increased carbon dioxide levels during their lifetime.

....

....

....

....

....

[4]

04 Where is the symbol below used and what is its significance?

....

....

....

....

....

[4]

Total

/ 8

Answers

03

3–4 marks	Three or four simple points of explanation or at least two points clarified in detail.
1–2 marks	One or two simple points of explanation or one point clarified in detail.
0 marks	No attempt or nothing worthy of credit.

Indicative content:

- *References to product lifecycle anticipated.*
- *Burning of fossil fuels to extract raw materials used in manufacture[1] and in transporting materials and products to factories[1] and shops.[1]*
- *Fossil fuels used to generate electricity to power machines[1] to make products,[1] and energy used by products in the home.[1]*

04

3–4 marks	Three or four simple points of explanation or at least two points clarified in detail.
1–2 marks	One or two simple points of explanation or one point clarified in detail.
0 marks	No attempt or nothing worthy of credit.

Indicative content:

- *The Fairtrade logo indicates that a product has been sourced fairly[1] with producers paid a fair price[1] even if it costs manufacturers more.[1]*
- *Shows support to farmers in having more control over their lives.[1]*
- *A commitment by manufacturers and consumers in the developed world[1] to support developing countries and their citizens.[1]*

3.3.3 THE WORK OF OTHER DESIGNERS

01 Discuss the work of **one** designer you have studied from the list in **Table 1**.

1. Harry Beck	10. Raymond Templier	19. Pierre Davis
2. Marcel Breuer	11. Gerrit Reitveld	20. Yinka Ilori
3. Coco Chanel	12. Charles Rennie Macintosh	21. Zaha Hadid
4. Norman Foster	13. Aldo Rossi	22. Elsie Owusu
5. Alec Issigonis	14. Ettore Sottsass	23. Karim Rashid
6. William Morris	15. Philippe Starck	24. Kusheda Mensah
7. Alexander McQueen	16. Vivienne Westwood	25. Aljoud Lootah
8. Mary Quant	17. Joe Casely-Hayford	26. Morag Myerscough
9. Louis Comfort Tiffany	18. Rei Kawakubo	27. The Singh Twins

Table 1

My chosen designer is: *Harry Beck.*

Harry Beck was responsible for designing the modern London Underground map. By profession, Harry Beck was a technical draftsman working for the London Underground office.

Exam tip

Discuss questions ask you to identify key points. In this question it is about **one** designer.

The specification only requires you to know about two designers.

Harry recognised that to produce a map showing the real-world position of train tracks and stations in relation to each other, would create a confusing and unclear map to understand. He recognised it needed to be simplified and easier to read, especially on the go while travelling. Having considerable experience designing and drawing electrical circuit diagrams, Harry used similar symbols and drawing styles to simplify what in the real world was very complicated to understand. Electrical circuits are drawn in vertical, horizontal, and diagonal lines crossing over each other where circuit tracks are not directly connected. Where a circuit wire is connected to another, then a dot is used to show this. Harry realised that train stations could be drawn and circles (dots) used where tracks stop or meet, so people can get on and off trains. He also used different track colours for the different lines e.g. Piccadilly line is dark blue.

[6]

Exam tip

Questions like this are marked using band descriptors. Read them carefully and aim high in the answer you give for Question **02**.

02 Discuss the work of **one** designer you have studied from the list in **Table 1**.

My chosen designer is: ....

....

....

....

....

....

....

....

....

....

....

....

....

....

....

....

....

[6]

Total

/ 6

☹ 😐 ☺

Answers

02

5–6 marks	Thorough, in depth, discussion about the work of **one** of the named designers.
3–4 marks	A good discussion about the work of **one** of the named designers.
1–2 marks	A limited series of statements about the work of **one** of the named designers.
0 marks	No attempt or nothing worthy of credit.

Note: Where more than one designer is discussed, only the best response will be credited.

3.3.3

THE WORK OF OTHER DESIGN COMPANIES

01 Choose **one** of the companies in **Table 1**.

Apple	Alessi
Braun	Dyson
Gap	Primark
Under Armour	Zara

Table 1

Exam tip

The specification lists companies that are linked to the specialist material areas. You should have studied **two** companies closely linked to your own specialist material area(s).

My chosen company is: *Apple.*

01.1 What is your chosen company famous for?

The design of mobile phones and computers.

[1]

01.2 Describe the features that have made your chosen company successful.

Apple have been at the forefront of technical innovation and development. They designed and manufactured products that were totally new and convinced people that they needed an iPod or a iPads to make their lives better. They were the company that introduced the smartphone with a big touch screen where you could use gestures and touch to dial numbers and control features rather than having to press buttons or use a stylus to touch the screen.

[4]

Exam tip

Look at the marking grid on the right-hand page to see how this response would have achieved four marks.

02 Choose **one** of the companies in **Table 1**.

My chosen company is: ....

02.1 What is your chosen company famous for?

....

[1]

02.2 Describe the features that have made your chosen company successful.

....

....

....

....

....

....

....

....

[4]

Total / 5

☹ 😐 ☺

Answers

02.1 One mark for a brief correct statement.

02.2 ***Indicative content: (Summarised responses - Add more detail if time allows.)***

Alessi: *Produced imaginative and innovative metal-based kitchen ware e.g., Juicy Salif. A focus on combining bright colours with stainless steel. Products were more concerned with form than function.*

Braun: *Developed small electronic products including razors and radios. Products were very functional, designed to be intuitive and easy to use e.g., obvious where to switch on.*

Dyson: *Innovative use of cyclone technology to make vacuum cleaning more efficient than bag technology had been before. Under the leadership of the founder, James Dyson, Dyson was concerned with innovative and original ways of solving long standing problems. Dyson first became known for the Ball Barrow, with its polymer green body and orange basketball shaped front wheel. It worked well as it was stable, easy to turn and had a low centre of gravity.*

Gap: *Famous for focus on distinctive every day and casual wear clothing. Developed a high-profile brand focused on ethical products, avoiding the use of sweatshops and child labour.*

Primark: *Marketed fashionable design at affordable prices aimed at the youth market. Focused on clothing and footwear so a full-dress style could be purchased in one shop.*

Under Armour: *A market focus on high trend sportswear. Products can be worn casually, but also used for intensive exercise. Products made good use of moisture wicking fabrics to keep you cool.*

Zara: *Focused on 'fast fashion' and being able to respond rapidly to new market trends and styles. They make affordable versions of exclusive, expensive clothing and luxury brands for the masses.*

3–4 marks	A good description of features making your chosen company a success.
1–2 marks	A limited description of features making your chosen company a success.
0 marks	No attempt or nothing worthy of credit.

Note: Where more than one designer is discussed, only the best response will be credited.

3.3.4 DESIGN STRATEGIES

01 Explain the term design fixation.

Designers become fixed on one design idea and cannot think of alternative solutions to a problem. Sometimes designers are afraid to make mistakes and a new or unique design may be seen as too much of a risk to take, so they keep designing in a style they are comfortable with. They play safe.

[3]

02 Describe the **two** following methods of exploring idea development.

Sketching: *It is possible to freehand sketch, sketch in 2D and 3D to share ideas with other people to develop a concept or idea. Freehand can be done quickly, anywhere, without special equipment e.g., a pencil and sketch pad. 3D sketching helps communicate a more real view of an item not possible in a flat 2D drawing. It is sometimes easier to identify problems, advantages and disadvantages by sketching them out and sharing with other people e.g., a client.*

Testing: *Materials can be tested to see how they will work before they are used in a prototype e.g., fabrics in a wash test. When a prototype is built, it can be tested to see how the concept works and if it needs further modification e.g., prototyping a circuit in a software programme or on breadboard. Testing allows flaws and defects to be identified early in production before equipment and materials are purchased.*

[2 × 3]

Exam tip

This type of question allows you to use knowledge and understanding from your specialist material area.

03 Explain why designers find it useful to collaborate. Give examples in your answer.

Designers work collaboratively to share ideas. Designers working with each other can 'spark' off each other and encourage new ways of thinking and approaching a problem that they might not do working alone. When collaborating, some designers may be electronic specialists while others might be material specialists. By collaborating, everyone plays to their strengths and help create a better product more quickly. For example, at Space X, lots of people collaborate in developing the concept design of the Starship. It is too challenging and demanding for one person alone.

[5]

Exam tip

The question asks for examples. This answer includes two detailed ones.

Do you remember?

Other design strategies you need to know about are: user centred design, system design and iterative design.

04 Describe the following **two** methods of exploring idea development.

Modelling: ....

....

....

Evaluating: ....

....

....

[2 x 3]

05 Testing is an important part of the iterative design process.

Explain the term iterative design.

....

....

....

....

[3]

Total /9

☹ 😐 ☺

Answers

04

3 marks	Two points with at least one clarified in detail.
2 marks	Two simple points in brief or one clarified in detail.
1 mark	A single brief descriptive point.
0 marks	No attempt or nothing worthy of credit.

Indicative content:

Modelling:

- *Simple models allow ideas to be realised and handled in 3D form.*
- *Uses low-cost materials to realise a concept.*
- *Materials are usually easy to shape and form to ensure rapid product development.*
- *Mathematical modelling to predict potential outcomes through simulation.*

Evaluating:

- *Evaluating against a design specification to see if the prototype satisfies the original brief and client needs and wants.*
- *Allows the designer to see which bits work well and where future development work is needed.*

05

3 marks	Two points with at least one clarified in detail.
2 marks	Two simple points in brief or one clarified in detail.
1 mark	A single brief descriptive point.
0 marks	No attempt or nothing worthy of credit.

Indicative content:

- *Designers use a cycle of continuous improvement.*
- *It is a cycle of prototyping, testing, gathering feedback and making improvements.*
- *Final products are released when a cycle has completed.*
- *A reliable, cost saving process that reduces manufacturing errors.*

3.3.5 COMMUNICATION OF DESIGN IDEAS

01 Below is an image of a toaster.

Complete a 1-point perspective drawing of the toaster in the space provided.

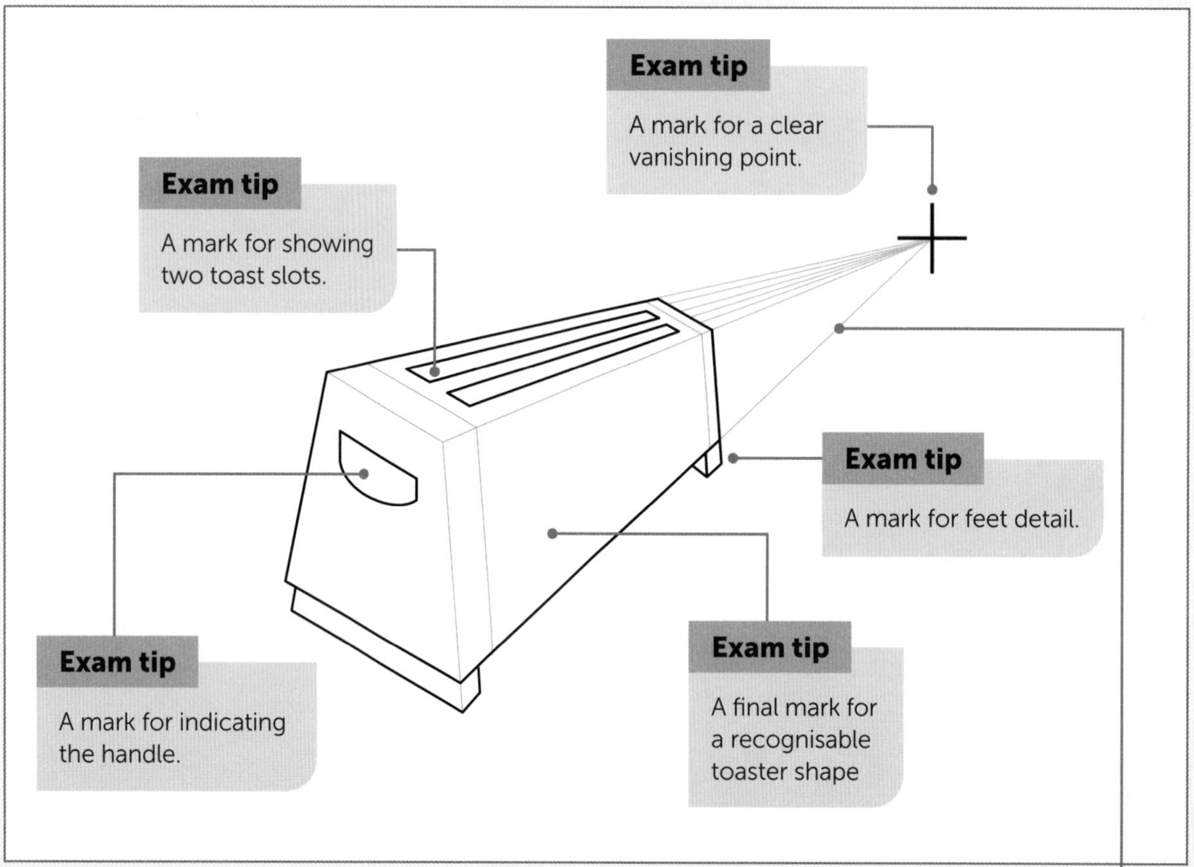
Exam tip
A mark for a clear vanishing point.
Exam tip
A mark for showing two toast slots.
Exam tip
A mark for feet detail.
Exam tip
A mark for indicating the handle.
Exam tip
A final mark for a recognisable toaster shape

[5]

Exam tip

This example is not perfect and that's ok! Examiners never look for a perfect drawing. They look for key features and points of understanding. A toaster could be drawn using 2-point perspective. Even 1-point drawings like this one may have some lines that help complete the shape, but it is not too important where they go.

Exam tip

Make sure that you always show the vanishing point(s) you are working to on a perspective drawing.

You can leave in faint construction lines to help explain your sketch.

02 Below is a drawing of a child's building block.

Complete the third angle orthographic projection by adding missing detail to the Plan view, Front view and Side view in the boxes provided.

[3]

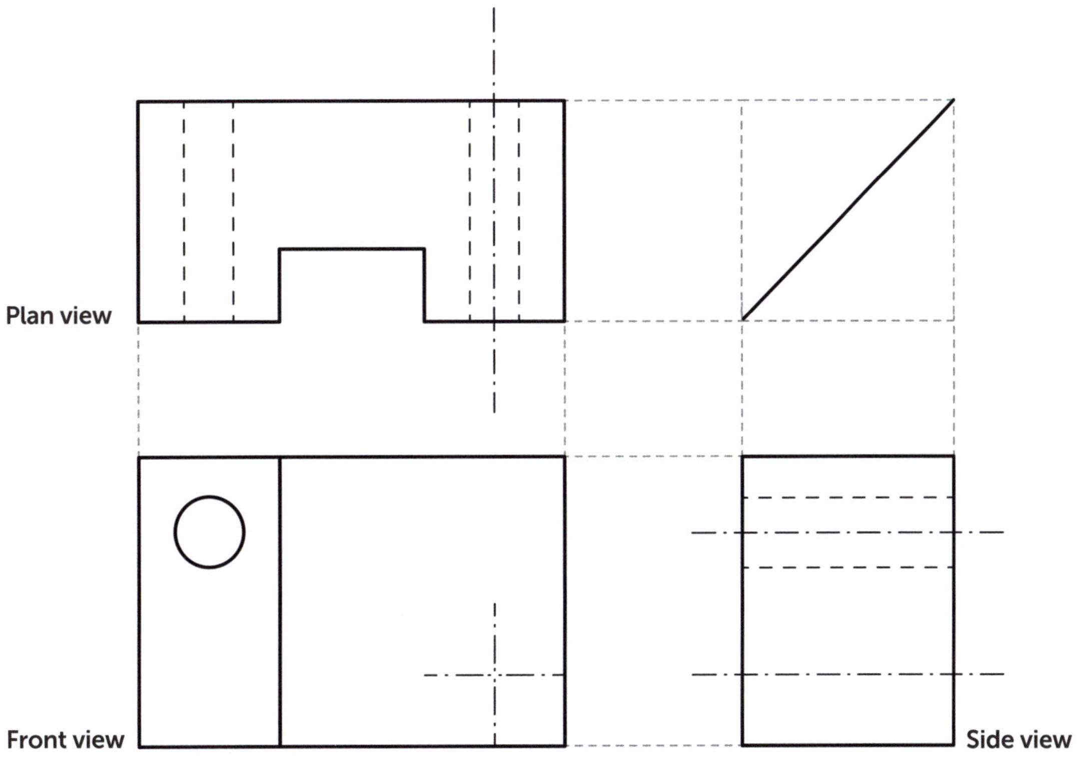

Total

/ 3

Answers

02 *Up to three marks from:*

1 mark	*Missing centre line on the Plan View.*
1 mark	*Missing centre lines on the Front View.*
1 mark	*Missing circle detail on Front View.*
1 mark	*Missing vertical line of Front View.*
1 mark	*Missing hidden detail lines on Side View.*

Indicative content:

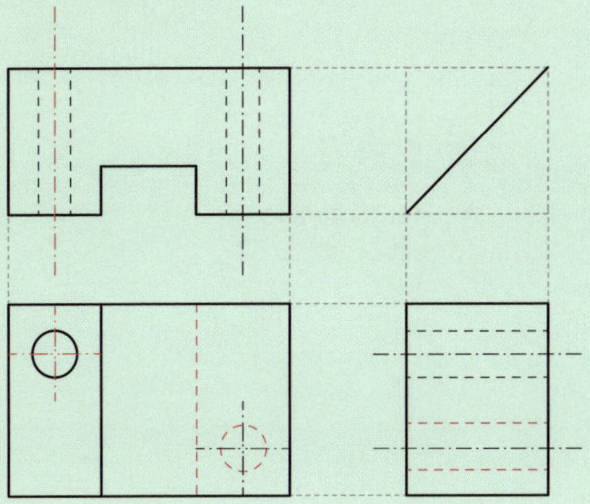

3.3.5 CONTINUED...

03 A drawing of an angle grinder is shown below.

03.1 Name the drawing technique used below to show assembly information for the angle grinder.

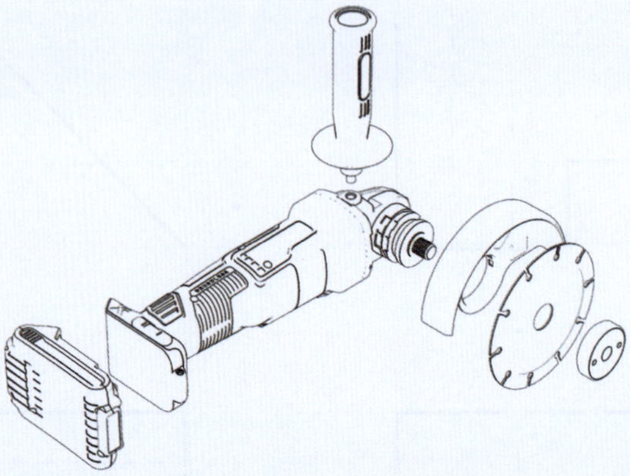

The drawing technique is: *Exploded drawing.*

[1]

Do you remember?

You also need to be familiar with isometric drawings and modelling.

03.2 Describe the benefits of using the drawing technique shown in **03.1**.

Exploded drawings allow a designer to show detail of how a product goes together to help with assembly.

Exploded drawings are used by manufacturers to help customers assemble and put together some products they may purchase e.g. flat pack furniture.

[4]

04 Show in the space provided, how you would indicate a working drawing had been produced to half of full or actual size.

Scale 1:2

[2]

Exam tip

One mark for correct format i.e. scale with numbers in ratio.

Exam tip

A second mark for correct order of 1:2

05 Explain why annotated drawings of prototypes may be considered superior to freehand sketches.

....

....

....

....

....

....

....

[4]

06 Draw the symbol used to show a 3rd angle orthographic projection drawing in the space below.

[3]

Total

/ 7

Answers

05

3–4 marks	Detailed explanation giving valid reasons why annotated sketches may be considered superior.
1–2 marks	One or two brief points giving benefits of annotated sketches.
0 marks	No attempt or nothing worthy of credit.

Indicative content:

- *Annotated sketches can be used to explain how the prototype functions.*
- *Notes added to sketches can clarify material choices, tools, and processes to be used.*
- *Dimensions and tolerances can be added.*
- *Annotations can help explain elements of a design that cannot be seen / are hidden.*

06

1 mark	*Symbol recognisable.*
1 mark	*Two parts of symbol drawn the correct way round for 3rd angle.*
1 mark	*Symbol drawn in proportion and using correct line conventions.*

Indicative content:

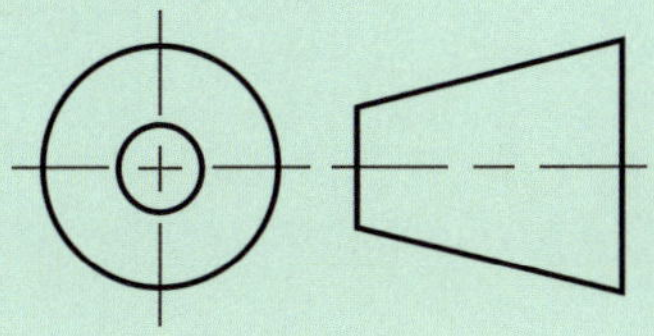

3.3.6 PROTOTYPE DEVELOPMENT

01 The product shown in **Figure 1** is prototype of a child's bicycle.

Do you remember?

You may be asked to suggest modifications to a prototype or how they demonstrate innovation.

Figure 1

Exam tip

This type of question could have multiple parts, where you are asked about the same product or products.

01.1 Analyse and evaluate the bicycle in terms of suitability of user needs and wants.

The bike has stabilisers on it meaning that it will help a child feel safe while learning to ride without a fear of falling off. The saddle and handlebars are adjustable to accommodate a growing child. This feature will also help parents save money as they won't have to buy a bike every time a child grows a bit.

[4]

Exam tip

This answer is good example of a response that considers both the adult and the child as a client in the analysis and evaluation.

01.2 Analyse and evaluate the bicycle in terms of its aesthetics.

The bike is a bright blue colour which will be attractive to many children. Manufacturers will no doubt sell bikes like this in a range of colours to appeal to all potential users and purchasers. The bike has reflectors attached to the wheels which are for safety. They can also make an attractive pattern for a child while the wheels are turning. All coloured parts are the same keeping it aesthetically pleasing to the eye and not a clash of lots of colours.

Exam tip

This part of the response is a safety point not and aesthetic point, but the candidate has evaluated how it could be an unplanned aesthetics feature.

[4]

02 The product shown in **Figure 2** is a baby walker to help a pre toddler learn to walk.

Figure 2

02.1 Analyse and evaluate the baby walker in terms of how it functions and its fitness for purpose.

....

....

....

....

....

....

....

[4]

Total

/ 4

Answers

02.1

3–4 marks	Detailed analysis and evaluation of several points showing a good understanding for function and fitness for purpose.
1–2 marks	One or two brief points of analysis and/or evaluation showing some understanding of function and fitness for purpose.
0 marks	No attempt or nothing worthy of credit.

Indicative content:

- *The walker is cushioned with soft materials,*[1] *so the infant is comfortable.*[1]
- *The walker has a wide base*[1] *and a low centre of gravity*[1] *for added stability*[1] *so the child should not fall or topple out.*[1]
- *The walker has some toys attached*[1] *so the child can play in the walker*[1] *and not become bored and want to get out too quickly.*[1]
- *The wheels are covered with a bumper*[1] *so as not to hurt another child if they get their feet in the way / reduce damage to skirting and furniture.*[1]
- *The walker is collapsible*[1] *so that it folds away into a smaller space when not in use.*[1]
- *The walker is made from waterproof materials / removeable fabric*[1] *so any spillages can be cleaned up / washed off to keep the product hygienic.*[1]

3.3.7 SELECTION OF MATERIALS AND COMPONENTS

01 Explain the importance of material availability in deciding what materials to use when making products. Give an example in your answer.

When making a product, the manufacturer first needs to make sure that appropriate materials to make it are available. If they are scarce or in short supply, this could lead to delays in production which could could impact the supply chain including retailers and the end consumer. Materials also need to be from renewable sources to ensure a long future of availability. Hardwood furniture manufacturers now tend to use sapele wood instead of mahogany to ensure longer term availability.

[3]

Exam tip

This answer fully answers the question as an example is given.

02 Outline how you would consider the cost of materials and components before deciding what to use to make a prototype of a design.
Give an example in your answer.

I would have to decide if I could afford the materials or if I needed to choose a cheaper form. If I was making a prototype, I would not have to construct it using the same quality of materials as the final product. Cheaper materials could be used so long as they allow the prototype to demonstrate what it needs to do. If I was making a dress, I could use a cheaper material to show what it would look like using toile rather than using very expensive printed high-quality fabric.

[3]

Exam tip

Outline questions want you to set out the main features or characteristics. You can include examples from any material area in your responses.

03 Explain the importance of choosing materials or components based on function when making a model or prototype.

When modelling, you often want the model to show what a final product or prototype will look like or how features will work. The material will need to be stiff enough to support its own weight and allow the model to be handled by a client if necessary, e.g., a model for a new kettle.

When building a prototype electronic circuit, sometimes you need to see how a real component will work so a designer may select the actual components to be used in a circuit and use them on a prototype or breadboard.

[3]

Exam tip

This answer has two good examples. The question only asks for one so the examiner will credit the best one. You won't get extra marks for a second.

04 Designers must select materials and components suitable for a task by considering different factors.

Function **Cost** **Availability**

Choose **one** of the factors above and **circle your choice**.

Describe how your chosen factor is considered when selecting materials and components.

Give an example to support your chosen factor.

....

....

....

....

....

....

....

....

....

[4]

Total

/ 4

Answers

04

3–4 marks	Detailed description of several points showing a good understanding of function and fitness for purpose. Example given.
1–2 marks	One or two brief points described showing some understanding of function and example of use to clarify response.
0 marks	No attempt or nothing worthy of credit.

Indicative content:

Function	Cost	Availability
• *Correct physical properties.* • *Correct working properties.*	• *Can the material be bought in bulk?* • *Cheaper material rather than more expensive final material.*	• *Scarce or easy to source e.g., extraction and transport.* • *Availability in stock forms.*

3.3.8 TOLERANCES

Exam tip

One point is clarified in detail to gain both marks.

01 What does the term tolerance mean when working with materials?

Material tolerance is the minimum and maximum limits of acceptability when deciding if a material is of the correct specific measurement for use in terms of dimensions, weight or resistance for example.

[2]

Exam tip

Some good example detail added.

02 Explain why manufactures make components and parts to a tolerance.

Manufactures make components and parts to a tolerance to make such they are within an acceptable size, shape, weight, resistance value or colour range to be used in a prototype or product. Manufacturers cannot afford to discard every component that is not a perfect size or fit. A component or part may still work perfectly well if it is a bit big or a bit small and discarding it would be a waste.

[2]

03 The component shown in **Figure 1** is an electrical resistor.

Figure 1

The brown, black and orange colour bands indicate the resistor to be 10 kilo ohms in value.

The gold band shows that the resistor has been manufactured with a tolerance of +/– 5%.

Do you remember?

Why are coloured bands used on resistors to show values rather than numbers?

Numbers may be too small to read on smaller components and there is no right way up for them, so a colour band can go all the way around.

Can you think of a problem with using colours for different number values?

03.1 Calculate 5% of the total resistor value.

10,000 / 5 = 500 or 500 ohms

[1]

03.2 Calculate the maximum and minimum sizes the resistor could be.

Maximum value: *10,000 + 500 = 10.5 Kilo ohms*

Minimum value: *10,000 – 500 = 9.5 Kilo ohms*

[2]

Exam tip

Don't forget to show your working.

04 What does the term tolerance mean when working with parts for a product?

....

....

....

....

[2]

05 The part shown in **Figure 2** is manufactured with two holes.

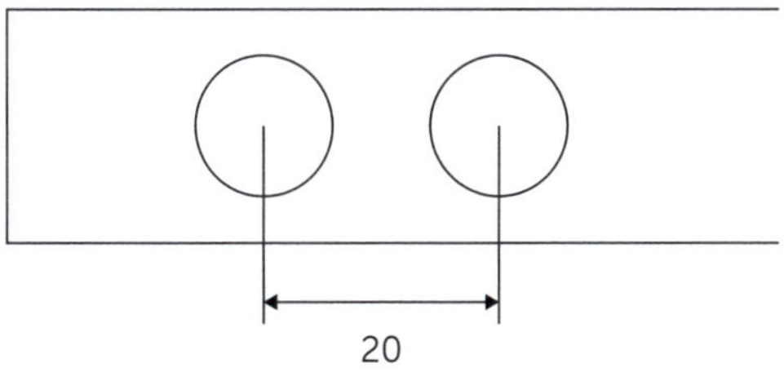

Figure 2

Both holes are drilled with a distance of 20 mm between their centres.

The holes are drilled with a tolerance of +/– 1mm off each of their centres.

Calculate the maximum and minimum distance allowed between their centres.

Maximum distance: ....

Minimum distance: ....

[2]

Total / 4

Answers

04

2 marks	Two simple points in brief or one clarified in detail.
1 mark	A single brief descriptive point.
0 marks	No attempt or nothing worthy of credit.

Indicative content:

- *The amount of acceptable error against the criteria.*
- *How big or small a component can be within a tolerance e.g., +/– 1 mm.*
- *How light or heavy a component can be within a tolerance e.g., +/– 10 g.*
- *How accurate its value is to a given number e.g., +/– 2 %.*

05

1 mark	*Correct max distance e.g., 20 + 2 = 22 mm.*
1 mark	*Correct min distance e.g. 20 – 2 = 18 mm.*
0 marks	No attempt or nothing worthy of credit.

3.3.9 MATERIAL MANAGEMENT

Do you remember?

Lots of the content you need to consider for material management has also been studied earlier in this book under production aids. For example, templates, jigs and patterns can also increase accuracy. See **page 66**.

01 What does the term tessellation mean?

Where a pattern is created without any gaps. Like nesting, parts to be cut are placed as close together as possible. Tessellation should have no gaps; nesting will have gaps as small as possible.

Exam tip

It can be helpful to use related knowledge (nesting) to get your understanding clarified.

[2]

02 Describe why it is important to tesselate in designing and making.

By tessellating when marking out parts on material, you use all the available material as efficiently as possible with no waste. This can avoid any unnecessary expense of buying extra materials and problems associated with the disposal of waste.

Do you remember?

Sometimes you will need to cut more material for each part where a joint overlap or seam allowance is required.

[2]

03 Measuring and marking out needs to be accurate.
Choose **one** term below and explain how it can increase accuracy.

Datum points	Coordinates	Reference points

My chosen term is: *Reference points.*

Explanation: *A reference point is a mark where all measurements are taken from. When a laser cutter's laser is focused, it is normally positioned in the top left corner of the laser bed as a starting point.*

Exam tip

This answer includes a detailed example to help with explanation. That's ok.

Alternative responses: *A datum point is a line or edge from which all other measurements and positions are taken to ensure consistency and accuracy. For example, when measuring a series of holes in a belt or item of clothing.*

A coordinate is a number identifying a point or position. When cutting something out on a laser cutter, this could be the location of a centre point of a hole from a given side or edge of a shape.

[2]

04 Two material management techniques are shown in **Figure 1** and **Figure 2**.

04.1 Name the material management techniques shown in **Figure 1**.

Figure 1

The technique in **Figure 1** is:

....

[1]

04.2 Name the material management technique for the fabric pattern shown in **Figure 2**.

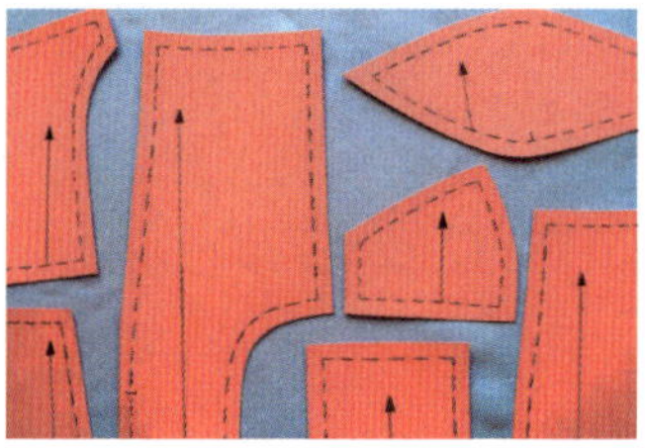

Figure 2

The technique in **Figure 2** is:

....

[1]

05 Describe why it is important to mark out parts as close as possible to each other when preparing to cut them out.

....

....

....

[2]

Total

/ 4

Answers

04.1 Tessellation.

04.2 Nesting.

05

2 marks	Two simple points in brief or one clarified in detail.
1 mark	A single brief descriptive point.
0 marks	No attempt or nothing worthy of credit.

Indicative content:

- *If you plan out lots of parts to be cut out on one sheet of material, you can reduce waste.*[1]
- *More efficient material use*[1] *minimises gaps between parts where possible*[1] *so more parts per unit of material.*[1]
- *Reduce set up times having to reload and prepare a new sheet of material for machining or cutting.*[1] *Reduces the need to dispose of waste.*[1]

3.3.10 SPECIALIST TOOLS AND EQUIPMENT

Do you remember?

You will have considered some specialist tools, equipment, and hand tools in **Section B** when you studied specialist techniques and processes in at least one material category or system.

Two new areas you need to consider are:

- CAD and CAM
- Safety

01 Give **three** specific items of Personal Protection Equipment (PPE) that are commonly worn to protect someone using tools and equipment in a workshop.

1. *Safety glasses.*
2. *Ear defenders.*
3. *Dust mask.*

[3]

Exam tip

Be careful and use words precisely on questions like this...

Avoid using words like 'mask' or 'goggles' which could mean a play mask or swimming goggles and may not be precise enough to get a mark.

02 Define the term 'CAD'.

CAD stands for Computer Aided Design.

[1]

03 Digital manufacture has several advantages over traditional manufacturing systems.

Describe **two** advantages of digital manufacture.

Advantage 1: *When using digital manufacturing techniques, work produced is likely to be more accurate as there is less chance of human error. Humans get tired and distracted and can make mistakes.*

Exam tip

Provide a detailed answer using key terms such as 'human error'.

Advantage 2: *A computer program can send information to a laser cutter or a 3D printer which can make lots of identical parts. There is no need to mark out each piece individually or draw round a template to make multiple copies. If the data file is accurate, the software will link directly to the CAM device to make exactly what is designed.*

Exam tip

Link your answers to earlier learning on production aids to clarify the answer.

[2 × 2]

04 Explain how heat proof gloves may be used to keep you safe when manufacturing.
Give **one** example of appropriate use in your answer.

....

....

....

[2]

05 Define the term 'CAM'.

....

....

[1]

06 Identify the specific piece of digital manufacturing equipment shown in **Figure 1**.

Figure 1

The piece of digital equipment in **Figure 1** is:
....

[1]

Total

/ 4

Answers

04

3 marks	One point explained in detail, **or** 2 points explained briefly **with** an appropriate example.
2 marks	One point explained in detail without an appropriate example, **or** one point explained in brief with an appropriate example.
1 mark	One brief explanation point or appropriate example of use.
0 marks	No attempt or nothing worthy of credit.

Indicative content:

- *Removing items from ovens, use with line bending machines and metal casting for example.*
- *Avoid scratches and burns.*
- *Provide additional grip.*

05 *Computer Aided Manufacture.*[1]

06 *3D printer.*[1]

3.3.11 SPECIALIST TECHNIQUES AND PROCESSES

Do you remember?

You will have considered some specialist tools, equipment, and hand tools in Section B. You will have also studied surface treatments and finishes. There is some overlap between Section B and Section C in the questions you can be asked.

01 Choose **one** of the surface treatments from the table below and explain why it is used for functional reasons.

Paper laminating	Wood preservative	Metal anodising	PCB lacquering	Fabric chemical fixing

Chosen surface treatment: *Metal anodising.*

Explanation: *Aluminium is anodised with cobalt to give it a bright blue colour, but also because anodising hardens the surface of the aluminium or aluminium alloy to make it harder wearing and durable. Aluminium and its alloys are quite soft and corrode easily unless anodised. Aluminium anodising is used on products like Maglite torches as they are used by the emergency services so must withstand lots of wear and tear.*

[4]

Exam tip

A detailed explanation of anodising. The answer would **not** get marks for reference to colour as the question is not about aesthetic finishes.

Exam tip

A good specific example, but not asked for in the question.

Do you remember?

Addition is a technical term to describe what happens when one material is added to another during construction of a prototype. Other techniques you need to be familiar with involve deforming and reforming.

02 Describe **one** process of addition used in the fabrication of a prototype.
Give **one** example in your answer.

A restaurant menu card made solely from paper or card will get soggy if a liquid is spilt on it. It will also stain and mark e.g. if food is spilt on it. By laminating the paper or card (addition by bonding a polymer wallet / cover), it will be a much more durable and effective product. The paper or card is placed in a plastic wallet and passed through heated rollers on a laminating machine to seal in the card. Addition enhances the working properties of the menu card.

[4]

Exam tip

Question starts with a clear example.

Exam tip

A detailed description of the addition process.

03 Choose **one** of the surface treatments in **Table 2** and explain why it is used for aesthetic reasons. Give **one** example in your answer.

Dyeing	Painting

Table 2

My chosen technique is: ....

Explanation: ....

....

....

....

....

[3]

04 Explain the term 'fabrication'.

....

....

....

....

[2]

Total /5

Answers

03

2 marks	One point explained in detail, **or** two points explained briefly.
1 mark	One point explained briefly.
0 marks	No attempt or nothing worthy of credit.

Indicative content:

Dyeing	Painting
• *Used for changing the colour*[1] *of a material by absorption.*[1] • *Examples: Fabrics / cloth,*[1] *yarn,*[1] *wood,*[1] *paper,*[1] *and card.*[1]	• *Used for changing the colour,*[1] *texture*[1] *or sheen*[1] *of a material by coating / adding a layer of colour.*[1] • *Examples: Wooden door,*[1] *metal car body,*[1] *silk scarf,*[1] *or signage.*[1]

04

2 marks	Two simple points **or** explanation of one clarified in detail.
1 mark	A single brief explanation point.
0 marks	No attempt or nothing worthy of credit.

Indicative content:

- *Assembling a product.*[1]
- *Putting a product or prototype together*[1] *using parts*[1] *or components.*[1]
- *Construction of a product or prototype using parts / components*[1] *that when brought together make a more sophisticated product*[1] *than the constituent parts.*[1]

PRACTICE PAPER

Information about the practice paper

Before attempting the paper, go through the previous section of the book and revise any sections that you aren't confident about. Use the face icons at the end of each topic to reflect on your level of understanding and make your own judgement of what needs more revision.

Now to the paper.

Section A of the paper is worth 20 marks.

- These consist of 10 multiple choice answer questions and a further 10 marks of short answer questions.

Section B of the paper is worth 30 marks.

- Several short answer questions and one extended answer question worth 8 marks.

Section C of the paper is worth 50 marks.

- A mixture of short and extended responses including a drawing question.

- You should do this paper under exam conditions.
- Aim to make the desk you sit at look as similar to that in the exam room.
- Turn off your mobile phone, music and remove all other distractions.
- Let everyone in the house know that you can't be disturbed for 2 hours whilst you do the paper.

!

You **will** need:
A black pen (and some spares)

HB pencil may be used for graphs and diagrams only.

Please write clearly, in BLOCK CAPITALS and black ink

Centre number .... Candidate number ....

First name(s) ....

Last name ....

Date attempted .... Time allowed: **2 hours**

GCSE DESIGN AND TECHNOLOGY

Unit 1 Written Paper

PRACTICE PAPER

MATERIALS

For this paper you must have:

- normal writing and drawing instruments
- a calculator
- a protractor.

INSTRUCTIONS

Write in black ink

Write your answer to each question in the space provided.

Answer **all** the questions.

INFORMATION

The total mark for this paper is **100**.

There are 20 marks for Section A, 30 marks for Section B and 50 marks for Section C.

The marks for each question are shown in brackets [ ].

This paper has 18 pages.

ADVICE

- Read each question carefully before you start to answer.

Final mark .... / 100 = ... %

SECTION A

01 What raw textile material is sourced from the creature in **Figure 1**? **[1]**

Figure 1

A Cotton ☐
B Leather ☐
C Silk ☐
D Wool ☐

02 Identify the smart material that changes colour under UV light. **[1]**

A Graphene ☐
B Photochromic pigment ☐
C Shape memory alloy ☐
D Thermochromic pigment ☐

03 Which form of energy generation uses a structure as shown in **Figure 2**? **[1]**

Figure 2

A Biomass ☐
B Hydroelectric ☐
C Solar ☐
D Wind ☐

04 Which **one** of the following metals is ferrous? **[1]**

A Brass ⬭
B Cast iron ⬭
C Copper ⬭
D Zinc ⬭

05 Which **one** of the following timbers is sourced from a tree as shown in **Figure 3**? **[1]**

Figure 3

A Ash ⬭
B Beech ⬭
C Mahogany ⬭
D Pine ⬭

06 Name the order of lever shown in **Figure 4**. **[1]**

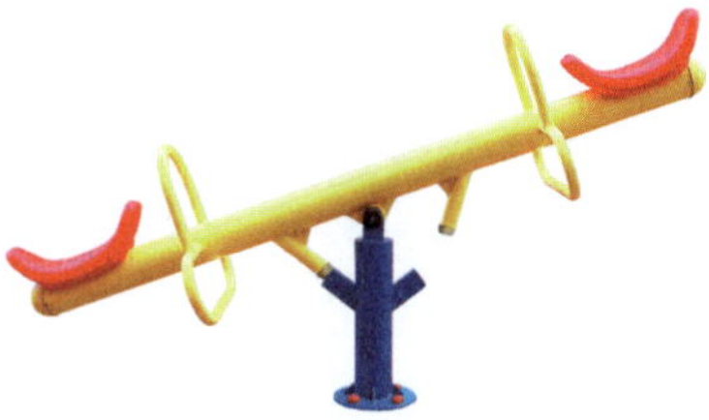

Figure 4

A First ⬭
B Second ⬭
C Third ⬭
D Fourth ⬭

07 What is the electrical component shown in **Figure 5** used for? [1]

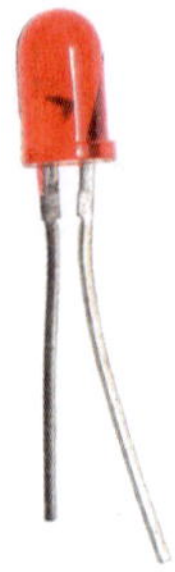

Figure 5

- **A** Detect a temperature change ☐
- **B** Emit a sound ☐
- **C** Light up ☐
- **D** Turn a device on or off ☐

08 A malleable material is one that: [1]
- **A** Can be drawn into a long length ☐
- **B** Returns to its original shape when stretched ☐
- **C** Shatters when dropped ☐
- **D** Will bend without breaking ☐

09 A mechanical product uses 7 screws in its assembly. [1]
A batch of 12 products are to be made.
How many screws are needed in total for all twelve products?
- **A** 48 ☐
- **B** 68 ☐
- **C** 84 ☐
- **D** 144 ☐

10 A new method of financing start up projects is: **[1]**

A Crowd funding ☐

B Efficient working ☐

C Upcycling ☐

D Virtual marketing ☐

11 Name **one** composite material.

....

[1]

12 Explain the term kinetic pumped storage system and why it is used.

Explanation: ....

....

....

Why it is used: ....

....

....

....

[4]

13 A set of six cushions are to be made. Each cushion uses 2.2 square metres of fabric. To ensure there is enough material, an extra 10% will be purchased.

How much material in total will need to be ordered?

Give your answer to the nearest whole metre squared (m^2).

Show your working.

....

....

....

Answer: .... m^2

[3]

14 Define the term 'continuous improvement'.

....

....

....

....

[2]

SECTION B

15 All products have forces acting on them.
Using notes and/or sketches, describe the **two** forces named below.

Compression: ....

....

....

....

[2]

Torsion: ....

....

....

....

[2]

16 Explain how materials can be reinforced using **one** of the techniques in the table below.
Give an example in your answer.

Lamination	**Webbing**	**Fabric interfacing**

My chosen technique: ....

Explanation: ....

....

....

....

....

....

....

....

[3]

17 Materials should be selected after careful consideration of environmental factors.

Describe **two** advantages in using recycling materials.

Advantage 1: ....

....

....

....

[2]

Advantage 2: ....

....

....

....

[2]

18 A torch manufacturer needs one on/off switch for each torch.

Pack size of switches	**Price**
50	£5.00
500	£45.00
1000	£400.00

A supplier only sells switches in **three** quantities at different prices.

Calculate the most cost-efficient way of purchasing switches to make 1200 torches.

Show your working.

....

....

....

....

....

....

....

£ ....

[3]

19 What is the meaning of the symbol shown in **Figure 6**?

Figure 6

....

....

[2]

20 Study **Figure 7** showing different sources materials.
Choose **one** source and answer both questions.

Trees	**Ore and rocks**	**Crude oil**	**Sheep**

Figure 7

My chosen material source is: ....

20.1 Name **one** specific process used to convert your material source into a useable form.

....

[1]

20.2 Using notes and sketches describe the process named in **20.1** in the space provided.

[5]

21 A life cycle assessment (LCA) considers the ecological issues in the design and manufacture of products.

Analyse and evaluate each of the ecological issues given below and how they impact the design and manufacture of products.

- Material sourcing
- Product miles
- Carbon footprint

....

....

....

....

....

....

....

....

....

....

....

....

....

....

....

....

....

....

....

....

....

[8]

SECTION C

22 Study the picture in **Figure 8** and the design specification below.

Figure 8

Design specification for the child car seat:

- Adjustable height.
- Adjustable side impact cushions.
- Adjustable cushioned straps.
- Large flat base.
- Lightweight construction.
- Reclining seat function.
- Removable soft fabrics.
- Rigid polymer body.
- Secure fixing into car.

22.1 Analyse and evaluate the child car seat in terms of safety features.

....

....

....

....

....

....

....

....

....

[4]

22.2 Analyse and evaluate how anthropometric data would have been used in the design of the child car seat.

....

....

....

....

....

....

....

....

....

[4]

22.3 Analyse and evaluate the child car seat in terms of suitability for the user(s).

....

....

....

....

....

....

....

....

....

[4]

23 A new floor is going to be fitted in a room of the dimension shown in **Figure 9**.

All dimensions are in metres.

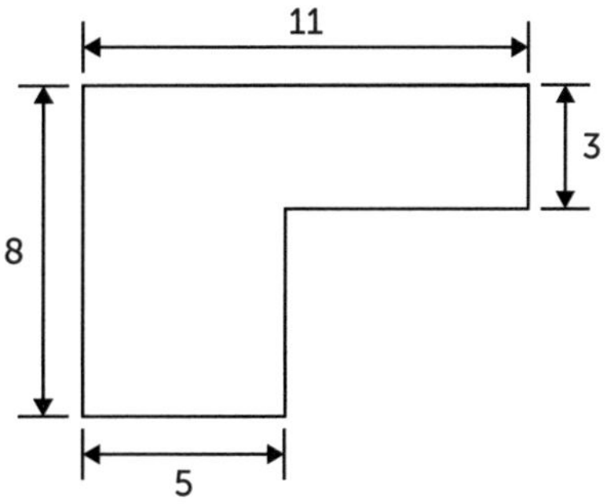

Figure 9

The new flooring material is sold in packs with 1.44m^2 coverage.

How many full packs will be required to cover the whole floor area? Show your working.

....

....

....

....

....

Answer: ....

[3]

24 Give **five** safety precautions a student needs to consider when using tools and/or equipment in a Design & Technology workshop.

1. ....

....

2. ....

....

3. ....

....

4. ....

....

5. ....

....

[5]

25 School children have been asked how they get to school.

The table below shows the type of journey and popularity of each journey as a percentage.

Type of journey to school	Popularity of each journey as a percentage
Car	45
Walking	30
Bus	20
Train	5

Complete the pie chart below by calculating the size of the sectors for bus and train journeys.

Show your answers by completing and labelling the pie chart.

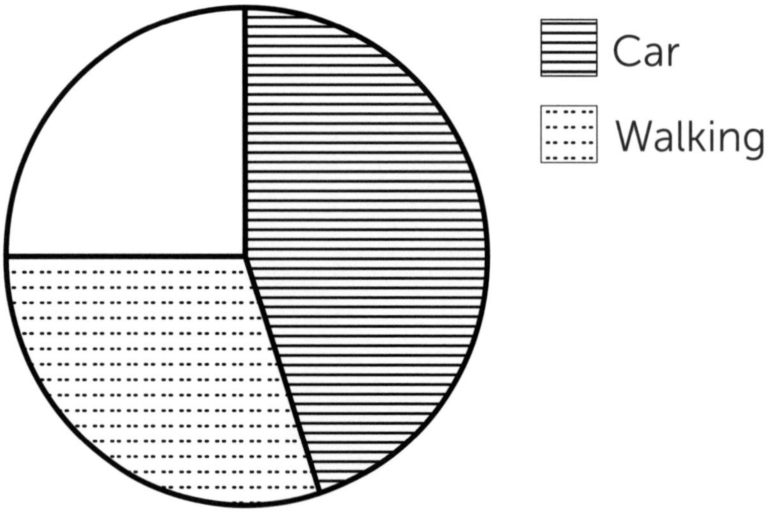

....

....

....

....

[3]

26 Below is a component drawing in third angle orthographic projection.

26.1 Complete the third angle orthographic projection by adding **two** pieces of missing detail on the plan view.

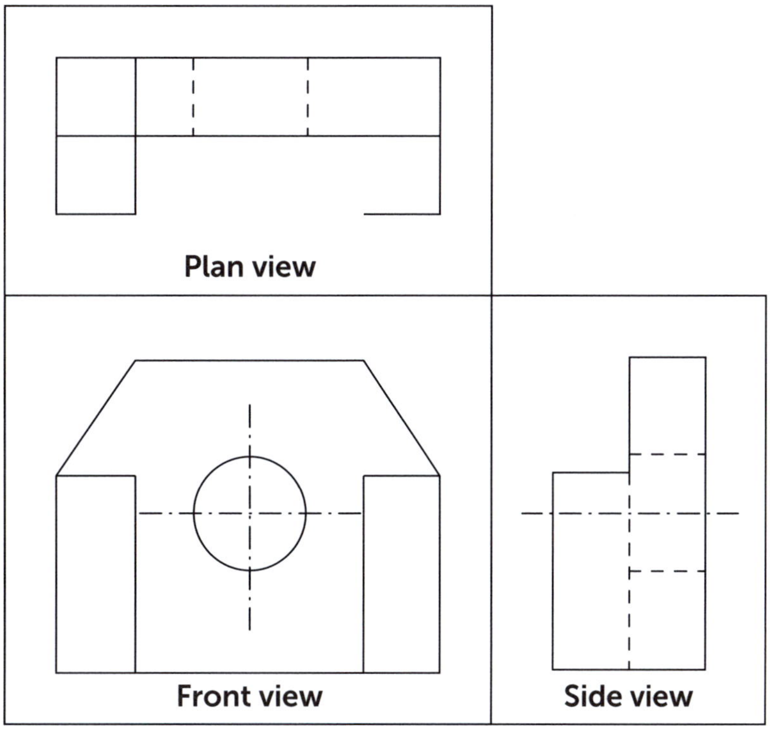

[2]

26.2 Complete the isometric drawing of the component on the isometric paper below.

[4]

27 System and schematic diagrams are used to communicate information.

Describe **one** advantage and **one** disadvantage of either type of diagram.

Advantage: ....

....

....

....

[2]

Disadvantage: ....

....

....

....

[2]

28 A new 2.5 litre tin of paint will cover an area of $32m^2$.

A tin that is partially used has enough paint to only cover $15m^2$.

Calculate in litres the volume of paint remaining in the used tin.

Give your answer to two decimal places.

....

....

....

.... litres

[3]

29 Choose **one** of the different pieces of machinery used in Design & Technology from the table below.

Laser cutter	**Overlocker**	**Lathe**

My chosen piece of equipment is: ....

Using notes and/or sketches in the space below, show how you would set up and use your chosen piece of equipment.

[6]

30 Give **two** reasons why surface finishes or treatments are applied to materials for functional reasons.

Reason 1: ....

....

....

....

[2]

Reason 2: ....

....

....

....

[2]

31 Discuss how user centred design can be used effectively to meet a client's requirements.

....

....

....

....

....

....

....

....

....

....

[4]

End of paper

PRACTICE PAPER ANSWERS

Section A

01 C – Silk [1]
02 B – Photochromic pigment [1]
03 B – Hydroelectric [1]
04 B – Cast iron [1]
05 D – Pine [1]
06 A – First [1]
07 C – Light up [1]
08 D – Will bend without breaking [1]
09 C – 84 [1]
10 A – Crowd funding

11 One mark for any of: concrete, glass reinforced plastic (GRP), carbon fibre reinforced plastic (CRP), plywood, MDF. Accept any other correct response. [1]

12 [4]

3–4 marks	Detailed explanation of kinetic pumped energy storage systems and why it is used.
1–2 marks	Limited understanding of kinetic pumped energy storage systems.
0 marks	No attempt or nothing worthy of credit.

Indicative content:

- Two reservoirs are connected by a hydroelectric system.
- Water falls past turbine blades by gravity when water is released from the top reservoir. It then collects in the lower reservoir.
- The turbine blades turn, generating electricity in a generator.
- At night, when electricity is cheaper and more readily available, water is pumped back up to the top ready for the next surge in demand.
- If there is a sudden need for electricity during the day, then power can be generated immediately and added to the national grid.

Accept other correct responses.

13 [3]

1 mark	$2.2 \times 6 = 13.2$ m^2 required
1 mark	$13.2 \times 1.1 = 14.52$
1 mark	14.52 rounded up to 15 m^2

NB: Award all three marks if answer is correct even if no method/working is shown.

14 [2]

2 marks	Two simple points of explanation **or** one clarified in detail.
1 mark	A single brief explanation point.
0 marks	No attempt or nothing worthy of credit.

Indicative content:

- Small improvements made to a product regularly over time.
- Something manufacturers do to try and stay ahead of the competition.
- Improvements to make production more cost effective and efficient.
- An element of the just-in-time / kaizen way of working to maximise efficiency

Accept other correct responses.

Section B

15

2 marks	Two simple points of explanation **or** one clarified in detail.
1 mark	A single brief explanation point.
0 marks	No attempt or nothing worthy of credit.

Indicative content:

1. Compression [2]
    - Two opposing forces moving towards each other.
    - A squashing / squeezing force.
    - Accept correct symbol if drawn for a mark e.g:

2. Torsion [2]
    - A twisting force where a clockwise turn opposes an anticlockwise turn.
    - A twisting / turning force.
    - Accept correct symbol if drawn for a mark e.g.

Accept other correct responses.

16 [3]

3 marks	One point clarified in detail **and** an appropriate example **or** two simple points **and** an example. **NB: Must have example for maximum marks.**
2 marks	One point clarified **or** one simple point and an appropriate example.
1 mark	One simple point **or** example of use.
0 marks	No attempt or nothing worthy of credit.

Indicative content:

- Lamination. Bonding a weaker material to a stronger material e.g. laminating card to make it less resistant to tearing, laminating layers of wood veneer to make plywood sheets (large flat stable boards).
- Webbing. Weaving of yarns to make a strong flexible fabric in more than one direction. Yarns can be woven. Car safety belts, retaining straps on a child car seat or pram.
- Fabric interfacing. Where an extra layer of material is added into fabric garments to stiffen a feature, e.g., shirt collar and cuffs.

Accept other correct responses.

17 Maximum of 2 marks for each advantage. [2 x 2]

2 marks	A detailed advantage description.
1 mark	A brief advantage description.
0 marks	No attempt or nothing worthy of credit.

Indicative content – Advantages of recycling:

- Saving precious natural resources, avoiding demand for new materials.
- Less destruction of ecosystems and animals when extracting new materials.
- Less damage to the environment though emissions machinery, to extract or to transport, producing fewer greenhouse gases.
- Fewer materials going to landfill and incineration.

Accept other correct responses.

18. [3]

1 mark	Pack 1000 switches x 1 = £400
1 mark	Pack 50 x 4 = £5 x 4 = £20
1 mark	£420 (Award all three marks if 420 given.)

19. [2]

2 marks	Waste Electrical and Electronic Equipment (fully correct).
1 mark	Some elements correct e.g., WEEE, mention of waste electronics.
0 marks	No attempt or nothing worthy of credit.

20.1 [1]

1 mark	One correct specific process.
0 marks	No attempt or nothing worthy of credit.

Indicative content:

1. **Trees:** pulping, seasoning, timber conversion.
2 **Ores and rocks:** smelting, electrolysis.
3. **Crude oil:** cracking, fractional distillation, polymerisation.
4. **Wool:** shearing, cleaning and carding, spinning, twisting, weaving

20.2 [5]

5 marks	Excellent notes and very clear sketches showing full understanding of the chosen process.
4 marks	Good notes and some clear sketches. Minor errors in understanding evident.
3 marks	Good notes and/or sketches showing some minor errors in understanding.
2 marks	Basic notes and/or sketches of the chosen process.
1 mark	One simple note and/or sketch clearly correct for chosen process.
0 marks	No attempt or nothing worthy of credit.

Indicative content:

1. Trees – Detail of pulping (paper and card products), seasoning and timber conversion, using saw mill / veneer.
2. Ore and rocks – Smelting at high temperature so that the ore runs out of the rocks.
3. Crude oil – Separating out different carbon elements using fractional distillation.
4. Wool – Shearing of sheep with detail of cleaning wool and spinning, twisting, or weaving.

See example diagrams on pages 48-52 and page 73.

21. [8]

7–8 marks	A very detailed analysis and evaluation of the 3 given ecological issues. Several examples used to support answer.
5–6 marks	A detailed analysis and evaluation of 2/3 given ecological issues. At least one example used to support answer.
3–4 marks	A basic analysis and/or evaluation of at least two of the given ecological issues. Possible examples used to support answer.
1–2 marks	One or two points liked to 1 or 2 of the identified ecological issues.
0 marks	No attempt or nothing worthy of credit.

Indicative content:

ANALYSE – Make a point.

EVALUATE – Look for candidate opinion in response.

1. Material sourcing
   - Expect consideration of deforestation to access raw materials and remove them.
   - Mining and drilling to extract materials and materials for fuel e.g., oil.
   - Farming – water used to feed livestock e.g., sheep for wool. Land clearance for grazing linked back to deforestation / desertification.
2. Product miles
   - Total distances involved in transporting materials/product from growth/sourcing to place of manufacture / point of sale.
   - Can products be made from locally sourced materials?
   - Transport from shop to the home of the end user.
   - Miles at end of life to dispose of and recycle.
3. Carbon footprint
   - Carbon produced by extraction or farming machinery used e.g., tractors, diggers.
   - Carbon produced by a product at any point during its life e.g., electrical devices using electricity. Possible analysis and evaluation of policies such as - turn devices off after use / do not leave on standby.
   - Energy used to dispose of/recycle a product at the end-of-life stage e.g. separation of materials, shredding and sorting.
   - Emissions during decay / when recycled.

Section C

22.1 Safety features: [4]

3–4 marks	Detailed analysis and evaluation of several points showing a good understanding of safety features on the car seat.
1–2 marks	Basic analysis and/or evaluation showing some understanding of safety features on the car seat.
0 marks	No attempt or nothing worthy of credit.

Indicative content:

Look for points analysed and then evaluated with an opinion to access the top mark band.

- Side impact cushions will protect the child if their head moves suddenly from side to side. This will prevent/reduce injury of the neck of the child. Will also offer some protection in the event of a crash and side impact.
- Seat is firmly secured into the car e.g., Isofix fastening to ensure firm positive 'click' on fitting.
- Padded straps will prevent them from digging into the child and causing bruising or cuts.
- Large flat base will stabilise the seat in the car and stop it from tipping over or sliding around. This feature could be improved with a non-slip material added to the underside.
- Rounded corners and soft fabrics to prevent cuts and abrasions.
- Adjustable straps to hold child in place.
- Webbing used as it is extremely strong under tension / in an impact.

22.2 Anthropometric data: [4]

3–4 marks	Detailed analysis and evaluation of several points showing a good understanding of where anthropometrics are used.
1–2 marks	Basic analysis and/or evaluation showing some understanding of where anthropometrics used.
0 marks	No attempt or nothing worthy of credit.

Indicative content

NB: Look for mention of size of the child's body.

Look for points analysed and then evaluated with opinion to access top mark band.

- Leg length of the child to inform the length of the seat base.
- Possible height ranges for any adjustments that might be needed to the car seat, so the child doesn't outgrow it too soon. These are expensive items so parents/carers don't want to keep replacing them.
- Waist dimensions to inform how long the lap strap needs to be and how much adjustment there needs to be.
- Head width to fit between side impact protection features.
- Possible mention of designing for a percentile range i.e., 5th to 95th percentiles.

22.3 Suitability for the user: [4]

N.B: User could be the child or the parent/carer of the child.

3–4 marks	Detailed analysis and evaluation of several points showing a good understanding about suitability for child/parent/carer.
1–2 marks	Basic analysis and/or evaluation showing some understanding about suitability for child/parent/carer.
0 marks	No attempt or nothing worthy of credit.

Indicative content:

Look for points analysed and then evaluated with opinion to access top mark band.

Parent/carer:

- Removable soft coverings in case the child spills something or is sick. It will allow parent to keep the covering clean, fresh and hygienic.
- BSI kitemark on the car seat somewhere to give the parent/carer assurance that it has been independently tested and is safe to use.
- Lightweight materials e.g. hollow, blow moulded polymer body to allow for ease of removal, install, carrying by parent or carer.

Child:

- Soft material for comfort. Doesn't rub on skin / no sharp edges.
- Anti-tamper catches to stop the child from releasing themselves from the seat.
- Adjustable features allowing for a child to grow.

23 Award full marks for no working if correct answer of 41 is given. [3]

1 mark	Total area = 5 x 5 = 25m^2 and 11 x 3 = 33m^2 = 58m^2
1 mark	58 / 1.44 = 40.27
1 mark	41 full packs will be required.

24 Safety precautions when using tools and equipment in D&T: [5]

1 mark	Any clear response (5 individual marks)
0 marks	No attempt or nothing worthy of credit.

Indicative content

Expect reference to a range of hand tools and equipment from all material areas in D&T.
Look for a clear link to a precaution e.g., wear safety glasses, (not goggles).
Responses likely to focus on three areas:

1. Preparing to use tools and equipment:
   - Selecting correct tool or piece of equipment
   - Inspect tool or equipment for any issues
   - Safety footwear if working with heavy objects
   - Tie hair back
   - Check position of emergency power cut off buttons
   - PAT testing confirmed on all electrical equipment
   - Make sure you are trained / know how to use tools or equipment.
2. Using tools and equipment:
   - Carry tools point down
   - Wear eye protection / face visor
   - Wear dust mask
   - Ear protection – machinery
   - Maintain 100% focus when using tools or operating equipment
   - Workpiece correctly secured or mounted if using machinery.
3. Storage of tools and equipment:
   - Return tools or equipment (if portable) to correct storage point
   - If a bladed tool or equipment, remove / retract blade
   - Clear away any waste material
   - Isolate power source if required.

25 Award full marks for no working if pie chart is completed and clarified correctly. [3]

1 mark	1% = 3.6°
1 mark	Bus = 3.6° x 20 = 72° Train 3.6° x 5 = 18° **Note:** same skill tested twice hence 1 mark.
1 mark	Correct sector line added to pie chart.

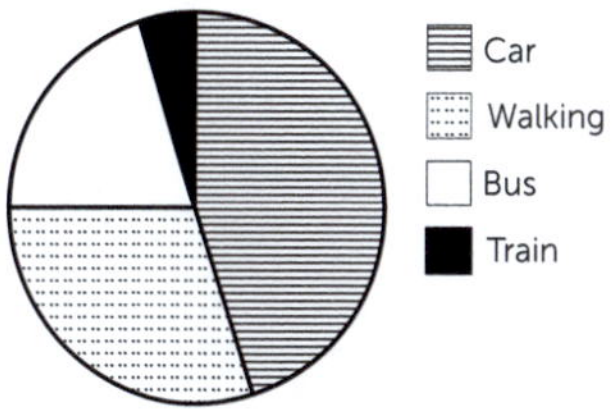

26.1 One mark for each correct line. [2]

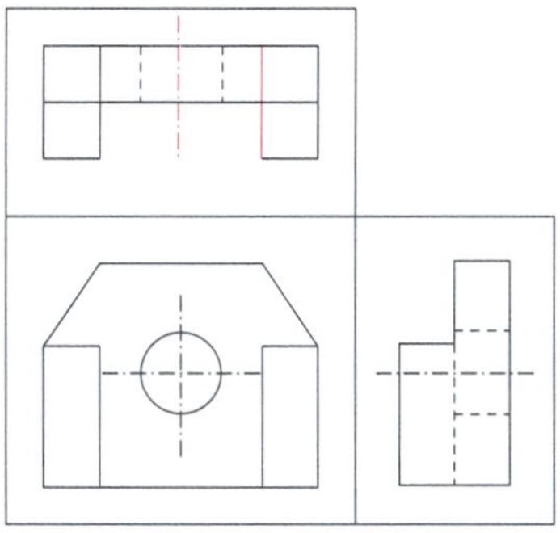

26.2 [4]

Indicative content:

1 mark	Correct attempt at a recognisable isometric drawing using grid.
1 mark	Two slopes.
1 mark	Recessed central section.
1 mark	Hole detail.

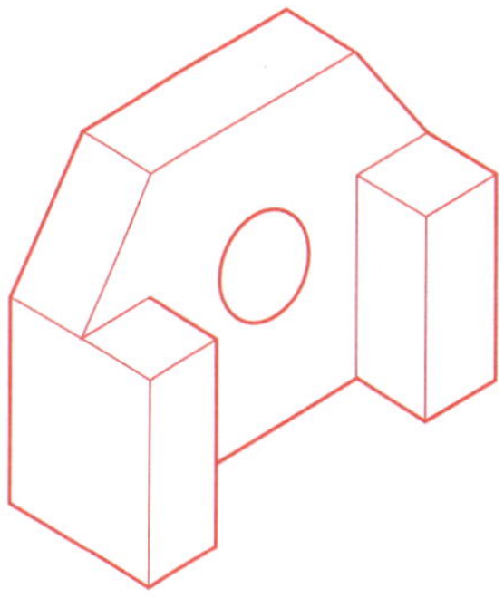

27 Maximum of 2 marks for one advantage and one disadvantage. [2 x 2]

2 marks	A detailed advantage or disadvantage.
1 mark	A brief advantage or disadvantage point.
0 marks	No attempt or nothing worthy of credit.

Indicative content:

System diagram	Schematic diagram
Advantages: • Simplify a diagram into input/process/output blocks. • You don't need to know detailed internal working of each block to complete a system diagram. • A lot faster to draw than detailed drawings of specific parts and components.	Advantages: • Recognisable symbols are drawn rather than having to draw out a picture of the actual component e.g. transistor. • A lot faster to draw than detailed drawings of specific parts and components. • Create logical diagrams that are easier to read e.g., London underground map.
Disadvantages: • They do not show any specific detail e.g. multiple parts or components needed in each process block. • Do not show how the different parts or components in a system are connected. • Lacking detail to make the system.	Disadvantages: • Symbols do not always look like the component or part they are meant to represent so it can be confusing. • Some symbols look very similar so it is possible for errors to be made in reading or producing a schematic diagram.

28 [3]

1 mark	How much paint per 1 m^2 = 2.5 / 32 = 0.078 litres per m^2
1 mark	How much paint for 15 m^2 = 15 x 0.078 = 1.171875
1 mark	Paint left in tin = 1.17 litres (to 2 dp.)

Indicative content:

Two marks max if not rounded.

If answer is correct and no working show, award all marks.

29 [6]

5–6 marks	A detailed description using notes / sketches of how you would set up and use the selected piece of equipment.
3–4 marks	A description showing some understanding of how you would set up and/or use the selected equipment.
1–2 marks	Simple notes or sketches showing limited understanding of the selected equipment.
0 marks	No attempt or nothing worthy of credit.

Indicative content:

Laser cutter

Set up	Use
• Check power settings for laser. • Check they are correct for material. • Check PPI (pulses per inch). • Position workpiece on the laser bed. • Use focus tool to focus the laser / autofocus. • Set datum/reference points.	• Make sure extraction is on. • Do a test cut. • Watch the laser to ensure it does not burn materials to be cut. • Send CAD file from suitable software program/file e.g. 2D design.

Overlocker

Set up	Use
• Machine needs to be threaded up before use. • Check rate of fabric feed. Needed to eliminate puckering, stretching and ripples in seams. • Do a trial run to make sure machine is doing what you want it to.	• Seam is stitched and finished in one go. • Stitch around the edge of fabric panels to produce professional looking seams.

Lathe

Set up	Use
• Select correct speed and feed rates (metal lathe). • Secure workpiece in a 3 jaw or 4 jaw chuck. • Secure face plate to workpiece (wood). • Position tool at centre line of workpiece.	• Select correct speed. • Use a live or dead centre to support a long bar extending out of chuck. • Use soluble oil coolant as required to keep tool cool, extend tool life and improve quality of surface cut. (Metal) • Remove chuck key. • Guard down (should be to work).

Accept other valid responses.

30 Maximum of **two** marks for each reason why surface treatment/finish is applied for **functional reasons**. Candidates may choose to use examples to clarify their responses. [2 x 2]

2 marks	A detailed functional reason.
1 mark	A brief functional reason.
0 marks	No attempt or nothing worthy of credit.

Indicative content:

- Applied to provide protection from the elements e.g., rain, snow, sun etc.
- Applied to make materials less prone to insect attack e.g., woodworm.
- Applied to make material less prone to fungal attack e.g., dry rot.
- Making materials less likely to fade in UV light e.g., fabrics, bleaching of polymers, fading wood.
- Finishes can be applied to protect against corrosion e.g., rusting and oxidisation.
- Improve the durability of a surface against knocks or scratches e.g., yacht varnish.
- Lubrication so one surface can move freely against another e.g., gear systems, lock mechanisms.
- Improve grip by rubberising / over moulding / knurling.

31 [4]

3–4 marks	A detailed discussion with good understanding of user centred design and **linked to satisfying a client**.
1–2 marks	Limited understanding of user centred design and **possibly linked to satisfying a client**.
0 marks	No attempt or nothing worthy of credit.

Indicative content:

- Look for reference to meeting client needs and wants.
- The client is involved throughout the whole designing and making process.
- The values and opinions of the client are sought at all stages of the design process to ensure the product meets their precise needs and wants.
- After product launch, client's opinions are still valued to ensure the product continues to meet ongoing requirements.
- Opinions gathered from the client can be used to help develop future evolutions of a product.
- Makes sure a product fulfils expectations and requirements of a specific client/user.
- Feedback on observations, surveys and questionnaires can be taken and used to inform designing and making first hand.

NOTES, DOODLES, GRADES AND DATES

....

....

....

....

....

....

....

....

....

....

....

....

....

....

....

Doodles

Grades

Target grade:

....

Practice paper mark:

....

Practice paper percentage:

.... %

Practice paper grade:

....

Key dates

....

....

....

EXAMINATION TIPS

When you practice examination questions, work out your approximate grade using the following table. This table has been produced using a rounded average of past examination series for this GCSE. Be aware that boundaries vary by a few percentage points either side of those shown.

Grade	9	8	7	6	5	4	3	2	1
Boundary	83%	76%	69%	60%	52%	43%	32%	21%	10%

1. Be aware of command words at the back of the specification. If 'describe' or 'explain' questions are given you need to expand your answers. To help you justify your responses, aim to include words such as BECAUSE... or SO... in every answer because this forces you to justify your point, so you get additional marks. See how well it works!
2. Explain questions such as "explain why this is the most appropriate..." do not require just a list of benefits. Instead you should identify the benefits and then expand each one, applying them to the scenario or context.
3. Full answers should be given to questions – not just key words. Make your answers match the context of the question. Where you are asked to give examples, always do so. Access to the higher marks will be difficult without examples.
4. Avoid simple one-word answers. Adjectives such as cheap, strong or quick are unlikely to gain marks unless these are justified. For example, "robots save money on wages" is not a strong answer. It would better to explain that "once the initial investment has been made, robots do not need to be paid wages but will require maintenance by more highly skilled workers".
5. Always include notes and sketches where you are asked to do so in a question. Support your drawings by using annotations and labels. Include detail such as processes and the use of any relevant tools or equipment.
6. Questions involving mathematics should be read carefully before attempting your answer. Misreading the question is a common way to lose marks on these question types. Show your working at every stage as marks can still be awarded even if the final answer is not correct.
7. Always give answers using the correct units, e.g. mm or kg, and to the correct number of decimal places.
8. In drawing questions, look out for key features such as holes or hidden detail and incorporate them into your responses using the appropriate line styles and techniques.
9. You are required to study at least one material area. However, not all material areas provide enough scope to answer all questions that may appear in an exam, particularly with electronic and mechanical systems. For this reason, it is recommended that you study more than one material area. This gives you more knowledge and understanding to draw from and apply to a greater range of questions.
10. 15% of the marks in the paper will test mathematics skills. You can check the full maths requirements in the most up to date version of the specification. This can be downloaded from www.aqa.org.uk.
11. Attempt every question, even if you are unsure of the question or the answer. Have a go. You might just get a mark or two, but you'll be guaranteed zero marks if you don't attempt a question at all.
12. Time your practice attempts in this book and in the examination based on roughly one mark per minute. A 4-mark question should therefore be given 4 minutes to complete. The real paper is 100 marks in 120 minutes. This will allow you 1 mark per minute with 20 minutes to check through things at the end.

Good luck!